CONVENTIONS AND DECLARATIONS

ENGLISH-FRENCH-GERMAN

CONVENTIONS AND DECLARATIONS

BETWEEN THE POWERS

CONCERNING WAR, ARBITRATION AND NEUTRALITY

(DECLARATION OF PARIS, 1856 - OF ST. PETERSBURG, 1868 - OF THE HAGUE, 1899 - CONVENTION OF GENEVA, 1906 - 2D PEACE CONFERENCE, THE HAGUE, 1907 - DECLARATION OF LONDON, 1909)

ENGLISH - FRENCH - GERMAN

Springer-Science+Business Media, B.V.

1915

ISBN 978-94-017-0052-8 ISBN 978-94-015-7601-7 (eBook)
DOI 10.1007/978-94-015-7601-7

ENGLISH TEXTS.

CONTENTS.

I. DECLARATION OF PARIS

APRIL 16, 1856.

The Plenipotentiaries who signed the Treaty of Paris of March 30, 1856, assembled in conference,

Considering: That maritime law in time of war has long been the subject of deplorable disputes;

That the uncertainty of the law and of the duties in such a matter gives rise to differences of opinion between neutrals and belligerents which may occasion serious difficulties, and even conflicts; that it is consequently advantageous to establish a uniform doctrine on so important a point;

That the Plenipotentiaries assembled in Congress at Paris cannot better respond to the intentions by which their Governments are animated than by seeking to introduce into International relations fixed principles in this respect.

The above-mentioned Plenipotentiaries, being duly authorized, resolved to concert among themselves as to the means of attaining this object; and having come to an agreement, have adopted the following solemn declaration:

1. Privateering is and remains abolished;
2. The neutral flag covers enemy's goods, with the exception of contraband of war;
3. Neutral goods, with the exception of contraband of war, are not liable to capture under enemy's flag;
4. Blockades, in order to be binding, must be effective — that is to say, maintained by a force sufficient really to prevent access to the coast of the enemy.

The Governments of the undersigned Plenipotentiaries engage to bring the present declaration to the knowledge of the States which have not taken part in the Congress of Paris, and to invite them to accede.

Convinced that the maxims which they now proclaim cannot but be received with gratitude by the whole world, the undersigned Plenipotentiaries doubt not that the efforts of their Governments to obtain the general adoption thereof will be crowned with full success.

The present Declaration is not and shall not be binding, except between those Powers who have acceded, or shall accede, to it.

II. DECLARATION OF St. PETERSBURG

$\frac{\text{NOV. 29}}{\text{DEC. 11}}$, 1868.

On the proposition of the Imperial Cabinet of Russia, an International Military Commission having assembled at St. Petersburg in order to examine into the expediency of forbidding the use of certain projectiles in times of war between civilized nations, and that Commission, having by common agreement fixed the technical limits at which the necessities of war ought to yield to the requirements of humanity, the undersigned are authorized by the orders of their Governments to declare as follows:

Considering that the progress of civilization should have the effect of alleviating as much as possible the calamities of war:

That the only legitimate object which States should endeavour to accomplish during war is to weaken the military forces of the enemy;

That for this purpose it is sufficient to disable the greatest possible number of men;

That this object would be exceeded by the employment of arms which uselessly aggravate the sufferings of disabled men, or render their death inevitable;

That the employment of such arms would, therefore, be contrary to the laws of humanity;

The Contracting Parties engage mutually to renounce, in case of war among themselves, the employment by their military or naval troops of any projectile of a weight below 400 grammes, which is either explosive or charged with fulminating or inflammable substances.

They will invite all the States which have not taken part in the deliberations of the International Military Commission assembled at St. Petersburg, by sending Delegates thereto, to accede to the present engagement.

This engagement is obligatory only upon the Contracting or Acceding Parties thereto, in case of war between two or more of themselves; it is not applicable with regard to Non-Contracting Parties, or Parties who shall not have acceded to it.

It will also cease to be obligatory from the moment when, in a war between Contracting or Acceding Parties, a Non-Contracting Party or a Non-Acceding Party shall join one of the belligerents.

The Contracting or Acceding Parties reserve to themselves to come hereafter to an understanding whenever a precise proposition shall be drawn up in view of future improvements which science may effect in the armament of troops, in order to maintain the principles which they have established, and to conciliate the necessities of war with the laws of humanity.

III. DECLARATION

RELATIVE TO PROJECTILES DIFFUSING DELETERIOUS GASES

THE HAGUE, 29 JULY, 1899.

The undersigned, Plenipotentiaries of the Powers represented at the International Peace Conference at The Hague, duly authorized to that effect by their Governments, inspired by the sentiments which found expression in the Declaration of St. Petersburg of November 29 (December 11), 1868,

Declare that—

The Contracting Powers agree to abstain from the use of projectiles the object of which is the diffusion of asphyxiating or deleterious gases.

The present Declaration is only binding on the Contracting Powers in the case of a war between two or more of them.

It shall cease to be binding from the time when, in a war between the Contracting Powers, one of the belligerents shall be joined by a Non-Contracting Power.

The present Declaration shall be ratified as soon as possible, etc.

IV. DECLARATION

RELATIVE TO EXPANDING BULLETS

THE HAGUE, 29 JULY, 1899.

The undersigned, Plenipotentiaries of the Powers represented at the International Peace Conference at The Hague, duly authorized to that effect by their Governments, inspired by the sentiments which found expression in the Declaration of St. Petersburg of November 29 (December 11), 1868.

Declare that—

The Contracting Parties agree to abstain from the use of bullets which expand or flatten easily in the human body, such as bullets with a hard envelope which does not entirely cover the core, or is pierced with incisions.

The present Declaration is only binding for the Contracting Powers in the case of a war between two or more of them.

It shall cease to be binding from the time when, in a war between the Contracting Powers, one of the belligerents is joined by a Non-Contracting Power.

The present Declaration shall be ratified as soon as possible, etc.

V. CONVENTION

FOR THE AMELIORATION OF THE CONDITION OF THE WOUNDED AND SICK IN ARMIES IN THE FIELD.

GENEVA, 6 JULY 1906.

CHAPTER I.

The Wounded and Sick.

Art. 1. Officers and soldiers, and other persons officially attached to armies, shall be respected and taken care of when wounded or sick by the belligerent in whose power they may be, without distinction of nationality.

Nevertheless, a belligerent who is compelled to abandon sick or wounded to the enemy shall, as far as military exigencies permit, leave with them a portion of his medical personnel and material to contribute to the care of them.

2. Except as regards the treatment to be provided for them in virtue of the preceding Article, the wounded and sick of an army who fall into the hands of the enemy are prisoners of war, and the general provisions of International Law concerning prisoners are applicable to them.

Belligerents are, however, free to arrange with one another such exceptions and mitigations with reference to sick and wounded prisoners as they may judge expedient; in particular they will be at liberty to agree:

To restore to one another the wounded left on the field after a battle;

To repatriate any wounded and sick whom they do not wish to retain as prisoners, after rendering them fit for removal or after recovery;

To hand over to a neutral State, with the latter's consent, the enemy's wounded and sick to be interned by the neutral State until the end of hostilities.

3. After each engagement the commander in possession of the field shall take measures to search for the wounded, and to ensure protection against pillage and maltreatment both for the wounded and for the dead.

He shall arrange that a careful examination of the bodies is made before the dead are buried or cremated.

4. As early as possible each belligerent shall send to the authorities of the country or army to which they belong the military identification marks or tokens found on the dead, and a nominal roll of the wounded or sick who have been collected by him. The belligerents shall keep each other mutually informed of any internments and changes, as well as of admissions into hospital and deaths among the wounded and sick in their hands. They shall collect all the articles of personal use, valuables, letters, etc., which are found on the field of battle or left by the wounded or sick

who have died in the medical establishments or units, in order that such objects may be transmitted to the persons interested by the authorities of their own country.

5. The competent military authority may appeal to the charitable zeal of the inhabitants to collect and take care of, under his direction, the wounded or sick of armies, granting to those who respond to the appeal special protection and certain immunities.

CHAPTER II.

Medical Units and Establishments.

6. Mobile medical units (that is to say, those which are intended to accompany armies into the field) and the fixed establishments of the medical service shall be respected and protected by the belligerents.

7. The protection to which medical units and establishments are entitled ceases if they are made use of to commit acts harmful to the enemy.

8. The following facts are not considered to be of a nature to deprive a medical unit or establishment of the protection guaranteed by Art. 6:

1. That the personnel of the unit or of the establishment is armed, and that it uses its arms for its own defence or for that of the sick and wounded under its charge;
2. That in default of armed orderlies the unit or establishment is guarded by a piquet or by sentinels furnished with an authority in due form;
3. That weapons and cartridges taken from the wounded and not yet handed over to the proper department are found in the unit or establishment.

CHAPTER III.

Personnel.

9. The personnel engaded exclusively in the collection, transport, and treatment of the wounded and the sick, as well as in the administration of medical units and establishments and the chaplains attached to armies, shall be respected and protected under all circumstances. If they fall into the hands of the enemy, they shall not be treated as prisoners of war.

These provisions apply to the guard of medical units and establishments under the circumstances indicated in Art. 8, 2.

10. The personnel of Voluntary Aid Societies, duly recognized and authorized by their Government, who may be employed in the medical units and establishments of armies, is placed on the same footing as the personnel referred to in the preceding Article, provided always that the first-mentioned personnel shall be subject to military law and regulations.

Each State shall notify to the other, either in time of peace or at the commencement of or during the course of hostilities, but in every case before actually employing them, the names of the Societies which it has authorized, under its responsibility, to render assistance to the regular medical service of its armies.

11. A recognized Society of a neutral country can only afford the assistance of its medical personnel and units to a belligerent with the previous consent of its own Government and the authorization of the belligerent concerned.

A belligerent who accepts such assistance is bound to notify the fact to his adversary before making any use of it.

12. The persons designated in Arts. 9, 10, and 11, after they have fallen into the hands of the enemy, shall continue to carry on their duties under his direction.

When their assistance is no longer indispensable, they shall be sent back to their army or to their country at such time and by such route as may be compatible with military exigencies.

They shall then take with them such effects, instruments, arms, and horses as are their private property.

13. The enemy shall secure to the persons mentioned in Art. 9, while in his hands, the same allowances and the same pay as are granted to the persons holding the same rank in his own army.

CHAPTER IV.

Material.

14. If mobile medical units fall into the hands of the enemy, they shall retain their material, including their teams, irrespectively of the means of transport and the drivers employed.

Nevertheless, the competent military authority shall be free to use the material for the treatment of the wounded and sick. It shall be restored under the conditions laid down for the medical personnel, and so far as possible at the same time.

15. The buildings and material of fixed establishments remain subject to the laws of war, but may not be diverted from their purpose so long as they are necessary for the wounded and the sick.

Nevertheless, the commanders of troops in the field may dispose of them, in case of urgent military necessity, provided they make previous arrangements for the welfare of the wounded and sick who are found there.

16. The material of Voluntary Aid Societies which are admitted to the privileges of the Convention under the conditions laid down therein is considered private property, and, as such, to be respected under all circumstances, saving only the right of requisition recognized for belligerents in accordance with the laws and customs of war.

CHAPTER V.

Convoys of Evacuation.

17. Convoys of evacuation shall be treated like mobile medical units, subject to the following special provisions:

1. A belligerent intercepting a convoy may break it up if military exigencies demand, provided he takes charge of the sick and wounded who are in it.
2. In this case, the obligation to send back the medical personnel provided for in Art. 12, shall be extended to the whole of the military personnel detailed for the transport or the protection of the convoy and furnished with an outhority in due form to that effect.

The obligation to restore the medical material, provided for in Art. 14, shall apply to railway trains and boats used in internal navigation, which are specially arranged for evacuations, as well as to the material belonging to the medical service for fitting up ordinary vehicles, trains, and boats.

Military vehicles, other than those of the medical service, may be captured with their teams.

The civilian personnel and the various means of transport obtained by requisition, including railway material and boats used for convoys, shall be subject to the general rules of International Law.

CHAPTER VI.

The Distinctive Emblem.

18. As a compliment to Switzerland, the heraldic emblem of the red cross on a white ground, formed by reversing the Federal colours, is retained as the emblem and distinctive sign of the medical service of armies.

19. With the permission of the competent military authority this emblem shall be shown on the flags and armlets (brassards), as well as on all the material belonging to the medical service.

20. The personnel protected in pursuance of Arts. 9 (para. 1), 10, and 11 shall wear, fixed to the left arm, an armlet (brassard) with a red cross on a white ground, delivered and stamped by the competent military authority, and accompanied by a certificate of identity in the case of persons who are attached to the medical service of armies, but who have not a military uniform.

21. The distinctive flag of the Convention shall only be hoisted over those medical units and establishments which are entitled to be respected under the Convention, and with the consent of the military authorities. It must be accompanied by the national flag of the belligerent to whom the unit or establishment belongs.

Nevertheless, medical units which have fallen into the hands of the enemy, so long as they are in that situation, shall not fly any other flag than that of the Red Cross.

22. The medical units belonging to neutral countries which may be authorized to afford their services under the conditions laid down in Art. 11 shall fly, along with the flag of the Convention, the national flag of the belligerent to whose army they are attached.

The provisions of the second paragraph of the preceding Article are applicable to them.

23. The emblem of the red cross on a white ground and the words „Red Cross" or „Geneva Cross" shall not be used, either in time of peace or in time of war, except to protect or to indicate the medical units and establishments and the personnel and material protected by the Convention.

CHAPTER VII.

Application and carrying out of the Convention.

24. The provisions of the present Convention are only binding upon the Contracting Powers in the case of war between two or more of them. These provisions shall cease to be binding from the moment when one of the belligerent Powers is not a party to the Convention.

25. The commanders-in-chief of belligerent armies shall arrange the details for carrying out the preceding Articles, as well as for cases not provided for, in accordance with the instructions of their respective Governments and in conformity with the general principles of the present Convention.

26. The Signatory Governments will take the necessary measures to instruct their troops, especially the personnel protected, in the provisions of the present Convention, and to bring them to the notice of the civil population.

CHAPTER VIII.

Prevention of Abuses and Infractions.

27. The Signatory Governments, in countries the legislation of which is not at present adequate for the purpose, undertake to adopt or to propose to their legislative bodies such measures as may be necessary to prevent at all times the employment of the emblem or the name of Red Cross or Geneva Cross by private individuals or by Societies other than those which are entitled to do so under the present Convention, and in particular for commercial purposes as a trade-mark or trading-mark.

The prohibition of the employment of the emblem or the names in question shall come into operation from the date fixed by each legislature, and at the latest five years after the present Convention comes into force. From that date it shall no longer be lawful to adopt a trade-mark or trading-mark contrary to this prohibition.

28. The Signatory Governments also undertake to adopt, or to propose to their legislative bodies, should their military law be insufficient for the purpose, the measures necessary for the repression in time of war of individual acts of pillage and maltreatment of the wounded and sick of armies, as well as for the punishment, as an unlawful employment of military insignia, of the improper use of the Red Cross flag and armlet (brassard) by officers and soldiers or private individuals not protected by the present Convention.

They shall communicate to one another, through the Swiss Federal Council, the provisions relative to these measures of repression at the latest within five years from the ratification of the present Convention.

General Provisions.

29. The present Convention shall be ratified as soon as possible. The ratifications shall be deposited at Berne.

When each ratification is deposited, a *procès-verbal* shall be drawn up, and a copy thereof certified as correct shall be forwarded through the diplomatic channel to all the Contracting Powers.

30. The present Convention shall come into force for each Power six months after the date of the deposit of its ratification.

31. The present Convention, duly ratified, shall replace the Convention of August 22, 1864, in relations between the Contracting States.

The Convention of 1864 remains in force between such of the parties who signed it who may not likewise ratify the present Convention.

32. The present Convention may be signed until December 31 next by the Powers represented at the Conference which was opened at Geneva on June 11, 1906, as also by the Powers, not represented at that Conference, which signed the Convention of 1864.

Such of the aforesaid Powers as shall not have signed the present Convention by December 31, 1906, shall remain free to accede to it subsequently. They shall notify their accession by means of a written communication addressed to the Swiss Federal Council, and communicated by the latter to all the Contracting Powers.

Other Powers may apply to accede in the same manner, but their request shall only take effect if within a period of one year from the notification of it to the Federal Council no objection to it reaches the Council from any of the Contracting Powers.

33. Each of the Contracting Powers shall be at liberty to denounce the present Convention. The denunciation shall not take effect until one year after the written notification of it has reached the Swiss Federal Council. The Council shall immediately communicate the notification to all the other Contracting Parties.

The denunciation shall only affect the Power which has notified it.

VI. CONVENTION

FOR THE PACIFIC SETTLEMENT OF INTERNATIONAL DISPUTES.

2d PEACE CONFERENCE, THE HAGUE, 18 OCT. 1907. I.

PART I. — THE MAINTENANCE OF GENERAL PEACE.

ART. 1. With a view to obviating as far as possible recourse to force in the relations between States, the Contracting Powers agree to use their best efforts to ensure the pacific settlement of international differences.

PART II. — GOOD OFFICES AND MEDIATION.

2. In case of serious disagreement or dispute, before an appeal to arms, the Contracting Powers agree to have recourse, as far as circumstances allow, to the good offices or mediation of one or more friendly Powers.

3. Independently of this recourse, the Contracting Powers deem it expedient and desirable that one or more Powers, strangers to the dispute, should, on their own initiative and as far as circumstances may allow, offer their good offices or mediation to the States at variance.

Powers strangers to the dispute have the right to offer good offices or mediation even during the course of hostilities.

The exercise of this right can never be regarded by either of the parties in dispute as an unfriendly act.

4. The part of the mediator consists in reconciling the opposing claims and appeasing the feelings of resentment which may have arisen between the States at variance.

5. The functions of the mediator are at an end when once it is declared, either by one of the parties to the dispute or by the mediator himself, that the means of reconciliation proposed by him are not accepted.

6. Good offices and mediation undertaken either at the request of the parties in dispute or on the initiative of Powers strangers to the dispute have exclusively the character of advice, and never have binding force.

7. The acceptance of mediation cannot, unless there be an agreement to the contrary, have the effect of interrupting, delaying, or hindering mobilization or other measures of preparation for war.

If it takes place after the commencement of hostilities, the military operations in progress are not interrupted in the absence of an agreement to the contrary.

8. The Contracting Powers are agreed in recommending the application, when circumstances allow, of special mediation in the following form:

In case of a serious difference endangering peace, the States at variance choose respectively a Power, to which they intrust the mission of entering into direct communication with the Power chosen on the other side, with the object of preventing the rupture of pacific relations.

For the period of this mandate, the term of which, unless otherwise stipulated, cannot exceed thirty days, the States in dispute cease from all direct communication on the subject of the dispute, which is regarded as referred exclusively to the mediating Powers, which must use their best efforts to settle it.

In case of a definite rupture of pacific relations, these Powers are charged with the joint task of taking advantage of any opportunity to restore peace.

PART. III — INTERNATIONAL COMMISSIONS OF INQUIRY.

9. In disputes of an international nature involving neither honour nor vital interests, and arising from a difference of opinion on points of fact, the Contracting Powers deem it expedient and desirable that the parties who have not been able to come to an agreement by means of diplomacy, should, as far as circumstances allow, institute an International Commission of Inquiry, to facilitate a solution of these disputes by elucidating the facts by means of an impartial and conscientious investigation.

10. International Commissions of Inquiry are constituted by special agreement between the parties in dispute.

The Inquiry Convention defines the facts to be examined, it determines the mode and time in which the Commission is to be formed and the extent of the powers of the Commissioners.

It also determines, if there is need, where the Commission is to sit, and whether it may remove to another place, the language the Commission shall use and the languages the use of which shall be authorized before it, as well as the date on which each party must deposit its statement of facts, and, generally speaking, all the conditions upon which the parties have agreed.

If the parties consider it necessary to appoint Assessors, the Convention of Inquiry shall determine the mode of their selection and the extent of their powers.

11. If the Inquiry Convention has not determined where the Commission is to sit, it will sit at The Hague.

The place of meeting, once fixed, cannot be altered by the Commission except with the assent of the parties.

If the Inquiry Convention has not determined what languages are to be employed, the question shall be decided by the Commission.

12. Unless an undertaking is made to the contrary, Commissions of Inquiry shall be formed in the manner determined by Articles 45 and 57 of the present Convention.

13. Should one of the Commissioners or one of the Assessors, should there be any, either die, or resign, or be unable for any reason whatever to discharge his functions, the same procedure is followed for filling the vacancy as was followed for appointing him.

14. The parties are entitled to appoint special agents to attend the Commission of Inquiry, whose duty it is to repressent them and to act as intermediaries between them and the Commission.

They are further authorized to engage counsel or advocates, appointed by themselves, to state their case and uphold their interests before the Commission.

15. The International Bureau of the Permanent Court of Arbitration acts as registry for the Commissions which sit at The Hague, and shall place its offices and staff at the disposal of the Contracting Powers for the use of the Commission of Inquiry.

16. If the Commission meets elsewhere than at The Hague, it appoints a Secretary-General, whose office serves as registry.

It is the function of the registry, under the control of the President, to make the necessary arrangements fo the sittings of the Commission, the preparation of the Minutes, and, while, the inquiry lasts for the charge of the archives, which shall subsequently be transferred to the International Bureau at The Hague.

17. In order to facilitate the constitution and working of Commissions of Inquiry, the Contracting Powers recommend the following rules, which shall be applicable to the inquiry procedure in so far as the parties do not adopt other rules.

18. The Commission shall settle the details of the procedure not covered by the special Inquiry Convention or the present Convention, and shall arrange all the formalities required for dealing with the evidence.

19. On the inquiry both sides must be heard.

At the dates fixed, each party communicates to the Commission and to the other party the statements of facts, if any, and, in all cases, the instruments, papers, and documents which it considers useful for ascertaining the truth, as well as the list of witnesses and experts whose evidence it wishes to be heard.

20. The Commission is entitled, with the assent of the Powers, to move temporarily to any place where it considers it may be useful to have recourse to this means of inquiry or to send one or more of its members. Permission must be obtained from the State on whose territory it is proposed to hold the inquiry.

21. Every investigation, and every examination of a locality, must be made in the presence of the agents and counsel of the parties or after they have been duly summoned.

22. The Commission is entitled to ask from either party for such explanations and information as it considers necessary.

23. The parties undertake to supply the Commission of Inquiry, as fully as they may think possible, with all means and facilities necessary to enable it to become completely acquainted with, and to accurately understand, the facts in question.

They undertake to make use of the means at their disposal, under their municipal law, to insure the appearance of the witnesses or experts who are in their territory and have been summoned before the Commission.

If the witnesses or experts are unable to appear before the Commission, the parties will arrange for their evidence to be taken before the qualified officials of their own country.

24. For all notices to be served by the Commission in the territory of a third Contracting Power, the Commission shall apply direct to the Government of the said Power. The same rule applies in the case of steps being taken on the spot to procure evidence.

The requests for this purpose are to be executed so far as the means at the disposal of the Power applied to under its municipal law allow. They cannot be rejected unless the Power in question considers they are calculated to impair its sovereign rights or its safety.

The Commission will equally be always entitled to act through the Power on whose territory it sits.

25. The witnesses and experts are summoned on the request of the parties or by the Commission of its own motion, and, in every case, through the Government of the State in whose territory they are.

The witnesses are heard in succession and separately, in the presence of the agents and counsel, and in the order fixed by the Commission.

26. The examination of witnesses is conducted by the President.

The members of the Commission may however put to each witness questions which they consider likely to throw light on and complete his evidence, or get information on any point concerning the witness within the limits of what is necessary in order to get at the truth.

The agents and counsel of the parties may not interrupt the witness when he is making his statement, nor put any direct question to him, but they may ask the President to put such additional questions to the witness as they think expedient.

27. The witness must give his evidence without being allowed to read any written draft. He may, however, be permitted by the President to consult notes or documents it the nature of the facts referred to necessitates their employment.

28. A Minute of the evidence of the witness is drawn up forthwith and read to the witness. The latter may make such alterations and additions as he thinks necessary, which will be recorded at the end of his statement.

When the whole of his statement has been read to the witness, he is asked to sign it.

29. The agents are authorized, in the course of or at the close of the inquiry, to present in writing to the Commission and to the other party such statements, requisitions, or summaries of the facts as they consider useful for ascertaining the truth.

30. The Commission considers its decisions in private and the proceedings are secret.

All questions are decided by a majority of the members of the Commission.

If a member declines to vote, the fact must be recorded in the Minutes.

31. The sittings of the Commission are not public, nor the Minutes and documents connected with the inquiry published except in virtue of a decision of the Commission taken with the consent of the parties.

32. After the parties have presented all the explanations and evidence, and the witnesses have all been heard, the President declares the inquiry terminated, and the Commission adjourns to deliberate and to draw up its Reports.

33. The Report is signed by all the members of the Commission.

If one of the members refuses to sign, the fact is mentioned; but the validity of the Report is not affected.

34. The Report of the Commission is read at a public sitting, the agents and counsel of the parties being present or duly summoned.

A copy of the Report is given to each party.

35. The Report of the Commission is limited to a statement of facts, and has in no way the character of an Award. It leaves to the parties entire freedom as to the effect to be given to the statement.

36. Each party pays its own expenses and an equal share of the expenses incurred by the Commission.

PART IV. — INTERNATIONAL ARBITRATION.

CHAPTER I.

The System of Arbitration.

37. International arbitration has for its object the settlement of disputes between States by Judges of their own choice and on the basis of respect for law.

Recourse to arbitration implies an engagement to submit in good faith to the Award.

38. In questions of a legal nature, and especially in the interpretation or application of International Conventions, arbitration is recognized by the Contracting Powers as the most effective, and, at the same time, the most equitable means of settling disputes which diplomacy has failed to settle.

Consequently, it would be desirable that, in disputes about the above-mentioned questions, the Contracting Powers should, if the case arose, have recourse to arbitration, in so far as circumstances permit.

39. The Arbitration Convention is concluded for questions already existing or for questions which may arise eventually.

It may embrace any dispute or only disputes of a certain category.

40. Independently of general or private Treaties expressly stipulating recourse to arbitration as obligatory on the Contracting Powers, the said Powers reserve to themselves the right of concluding new Agreements, general or particular, with a view to extending compulsory arbitration to all cases which they may consider it possible to submit to it.

CHAPTER II.

The Permanent Court of Arbitration.

41. With the object of facilitating an inmediate recourse to arbitration for international differences, which it has not been possible to settle by diplomacy, the Contracting Powers undertake to maintain the Permanent Court of Arbitration, as established by the First Peace Conference, accessible at all times, and operating, unless otherwise stipulated by the parties, in accordance with the rules of procedure inserted in the present Convention.

42. The Permanent Court is competent for all arbitration cases, unless the parties agree to institute a special Tribunal.

43. The Permanent Court sits at The Hague.

An International Bureau serves as registry for the Court. It is the channel for communications relative to the meetings of the Court; it has charge of the archives and conducts all the administrative business.

The Contracting Powers undertake to communicate to the Bureau, as soon as possible, a certified copy of any conditions of arbitration arrived at between them and of any Award concerning them delivered by a special Tribunal.

They likewise undertake to communicate to the Bureau the laws, regulations, and documents eventually showing the execution of the Awards given by the Court.

44. Each Contracting Power selects four persons at the most, of known competency in questions of international law, of the highest moral reputation, and disposed to accept the duties of Arbitrator.

The persons thus selected are inscribed, as members of the Court, in a list which shall be notified to all the Contracting Powers by the Bureau.

Any alternation in the list of Arbitrators is brought by the Bureau to the knowledge of the Contracting Powers.

Two or more Powers may agree on the selection in common of one or more members.

The same person can be selected by different Powers. The members of the Court are appointed for a term of six years. These appointments are renewable.

Should a member of the Court die or resign, the same procedure is followed for filling the vacancy as was followed for appointing him. In this case the appointment is made for a fresh period of six years.

45. When the Contracting Powers wish to have recourse to the Permanent Court for the settlement of a difference which has arisen between them, the Arbitrators called upon to form the Tribunal with jurisdiction to decide this difference must be chosen from the general list of members of the Court.

Failing the direct agreement of the parties on the composition of the Arbitration Tribunal, the following course shall be pursued:—

Each party appoints two Arbitrators, of whom one only can be its national or chosen from among the persons selected by it as members of the Permanent Court. These Arbitrators together choose an Umpire.

If the votes are equally divided, the choice of the Umpire is intrusted to a third Power, selected by the parties by common accord.

If an agreement is not arrived at on this subject each party selects a different Power, and the choice of the Umpire is made in concert by the Powers thus selected.

If, within two months' time, these two Powers cannot come to an agreement, each of them presents two candidates taken from the list of members of the Permanent Court, exclusive of the members selected by parties and not being nationals of either of them. Drawing lots determines which of the candidates thus presented shall be Umpire.

46. The Tribunal being thus composed, the parties notify to the Bureau their determination to have recourse to the Court, the text of their „Compromis," and the names of the Arbitrators.

The Bureau communicates without delay to each Arbitrator the „Compromis," and the names of the other members of the Tribunal.

The Tribunal assembles at the date fixed by the parties. The Bureau makes the necessary arrangements for the meeting.

The members of the Tribunal, in the exercise of their duties and out of their own country, enjoy diplomatic privileges and immunities.

47. The Bureau is authorized to place its offices and staff at the disposal of the Contracting Powers for the use of any special Board of Arbitration.

The jurisdiction of the Permanent Court may, within the conditions laid down in the regulations, be extended to disputes between non-Contracting Powers or between Contracting Powers and non-Contracting Powers, if the parties are agreed on recourse to this Tribunal.

48. The Contracting Powers consider it their duty, if a serious dispute threatens to break out between two or more of them, to remind these latter that the Permanent Court is open to them.

Consequently, they declare that the fact of reminding the parties at variance of the provisions of the present Convention, and the advice given to them, in the highest interests of peace, to have recourse to the Permanent Court, can only be regarded as friendly actions.

In case of dispute between two Powers, one of them can always address to the International Bureau a note containing a declaration that it would be ready to submit the dispute to arbitration.

The Bureau must at once inform the other Power of the declaration.

49. The Permanent Administrative Council, composed of the Diplomatic Representatives of the Contracting Powers accredited to The Hague and of the Netherland Minister for Foreign Affairs, who will act as President, is charged with the direction and control of the International Bureau.

The Council settles its rules of procedure and all other necessary regulations.

It decides all questions of administration which may arise with regard to the operations of the Court.

It has entire control over the appointment, suspension, or dismissal of the officials and employés of the Bureau.

It fixes the payments and salaries, and controls the general expenditure.

At meetings duly summoned the presence of nine members is sufficient to render valid the discussions of the Council. The decisions are taken by a majority of votes.

The Council communicates to the Contracting Powers without delay the regulations adopted by it. It furnishes them with an annual Report on the labours of the Court, the working of the administration, and the expenditure. The Report likewise contains a résumé of what is important in the documents communicated to the Bureau by the Powers in virtue of Article 43, paragraphs 3 and 4.

50. The expenses of the Bureau shall be borne by the Contracting Powers in the proportion fixed for the International Bureau of the Universal Postal Union.

The expenses to be charged to the adhering Powers shall be reckoned from the date on which their adhesion comes into force.

CHAPTER III.

Arbitration Procedure.

51. With a view to encouraging the development of arbitration, the Contracting Powers have agreed on the following rules, which are applicable to arbitration procedure, unless other rules have been agreed on by the parties.

52. The Powers which have recourse to arbitration sign a „Compromis," in which the subject of the dispute is clearly defined, the time allowed for appointing Arbitrators, the form, order, and time in which the communication referred to in Article **63** must be made, and the amount of the sum which each party must deposit in advance to defray the expenses.

The „Compromis" likewise defines, if there is occasion, the manner of appointing Arbitrators, any special powers which may eventually belong to the Tribunal, where it shall meet, the language it shall use, and the languages the employment of which shall be authorized before it, and, generally speaking, all the conditions on which the parties are agreed.

53. The Permanent Court is competent to settle the „Compromis," if the parties are agreed to have recourse to it for the purpose.

It is similarly competent, even if the request is only made by one of the parties, when all attempts to reach an understanding though the diplomatic channel have failed, in the case of:—

1. A dispute covered by a general Treaty of Arbitration concluded or renewed after the present Convention has come into force, and providing for a „Compromis" in all disputes and not either explicitly or implicitly excluding the settlement of the „Compromis" from the competence of the Court. Recourse cannot, however, be had to the Court if the other party declares that in its opinion the dispute does not belong to the category of disputes which, can be submitted to compulsory arbitration, unless the Treaty of Arbitration confers upon the Arbitration Tribunal the power of deciding this preliminary question.

2. A dispute arising from contract-debts claimed from one Power by

another Power as due to its nationals, and for the settlement of which the offer of arbitration has been accepted. This arrangement is not applicable if acceptance is subject to the condition that the „Compromis" should be settled in some other way.

54. In the cases contemplated in the preceding Article, the „Compromis" shall be settled by a Commission consisting of five members selected in the manner arranged for in Article 45, paragraphs 3 to 6.

The fifth member is President of the Commission *ex officio.*

55. The duties of Arbitrator may be conferred on one Arbitrator alone or on several Arbitrators selected by the parties as they please, or chosen by them from the members of the Permanent Court of Arbitration established by the present Convention.

Failing the constitution of the Tribunal by direct agreement between the parties, the course referred to in Article 45, paragraphs 3 to 6, is followed.

56. When a Sovereign or the Chief of a State is chosen as Arbitrator, the arbitration precedure is settled by him.

57. The Umpire is President of the Tribunal *ex officio.*

When the Tribunal does not include an Umpire, it appoints its own President.

58. When the „Compromis" is settled by a Commission, as contemplated in Article **54**, and in the absence of an agreement to the contrary, the Commission itself shall form the Arbitration Tribunal.

59. Should one of the Arbitrators either die, retire, or be unable for any reason whatever to discharge his functions, the same procedure is followed for filling the vacancy as was followed for appointing him.

60. The Tribunal sits at The Hague, unless some other place is selected by the parties.

The Tribunal can only sit in the territory of a third Power with the latter's consent.

The place of meeting once fixed cannot be altered by the Tribunal, except with the consent of the parties.

61. If the question as to what languages are to be used has not been settled by the „Compromis," it shall be decided by the Tribunal.

62. The parties are entitled to appoint special agents to attend the Tribunal to act as intermediaries between themselves and the Tribunal.

They are further authorized to retain for the defence of their rights and interests before the Tribunal counsel or advocates appointed by themselves for this purpose.

The members of the Permanent Court may not act as agents, counsel, or advocates except on behalf of the Power which appointed them members of the Court.

63. As a general rule, arbitration procedure comprises two distinct phases: pleadings and oral discussions.

The pleadings consist in the communication by the respective agents to the members of the Tribunal and the opposite party of cases, counter-cases, and, if necessary, of replies; the parties annex thereto all papers and documents called for in the case. This communication shall be made either directly or through the intermediary of the International Bureau, in the order and within the time fixed by the „Compromis."

The time fixed by the „Compromis" may be extended by mutual agreement by the parties, or by the Tribunal when the latter considers it necessary for the purpose of reaching a just decision.

The discussions consist in the oral development before the Tribunal of the arguments of the parties.

64. A certified copy of every document produced by one party must be communicated to the other party.

65. Unless special circumstances arise, the Tribunal does not meet until the pleadings are closed.

66. The discussions are under the control of the President.

They are only public if it be so decided by the Tribunal, with the assent of the parties.

They are recorded in minutes drawn up by the Secretaries appointed by the President. These minutes are signed by the President and by one of the Secretaries and alone have an authentic character.

67. After the close of the pleadings, the Tribunal is entitled to refuse discussion of all new papers or documents which one of the parties may wish to submit to it without the consent of the other party.

68. The Tribunal is free to take into consideration new papers or documents to which its attention may be drawn by the agents or counsel of the parties.

In this case, the Tribunal has the right to require the production of these papers or documents, but is obliged to make them known to the opposite party.

69. The Tribunal can, besides, require from the agents of the parties the production of all papers, and can demand all necessary explanations. In case of refusal the Tribunal takes note of it.

70. The agents and the counsel of the parties are authorized to present orally to the Tribunal all the arguments they may consider expedient in defence of their case.

71. They are entitled to raise objections and points. The decisions of the Tribunal on these points are final and cannot form the subject of any subsequent discussion.

72. The members of the Tribunal are entitled to put questions to the agents and counsel of the parties, and to ask them for explanations on doubtful points.

Neither the questions put, nor the remarks made by members of the Tribunal in the course of the discussions, can be regarded as an expression of opinion by the Tribunal in general or by its members in particular.

73. The Tribunal is authorized to declare its competence in interpreting the „Compromis," as well as the other Treaties which may be invoked, and in applying the principles of law.

74. The Tribunal is entitled to issue rules of procedure for the conduct of the case, to decide the forms, order, and time in which each party must conclude its arguments, and to arrange all the formalities required for dealing with the evidence.

75. The parties undertake to supply the Tribunal, as fully as they consider possible, with all the information required for deciding the case.

76. For all notices which the Tribunal has to serve in the territory of a third Contracting Power, the Tribunal shall apply direct to the Government of that Power. The same rule applies in the case of steps being taken to procure evidence on the spot.

The requests for this purpose are to be executed as far as the means at the disposal of the Power applied to under its municipal law allow. They cannot be rejected unless the Power in question considers them calculated to impair its own sovereign rights or its safety.

The Court will equally be always entitled to act through the Power on whose territory it sits.

77. When the agents and counsel of the parties have submitted all the explanations and evidence in support of their case the President shall declare the discussion closed.

78. The Tribunal considers its decisions in private and the proceedings remain secret.

All questions are decided by a majority of the members of the Tribunal.

79. The Award must give the reasons on which it is based. It contains the names of the Arbitrators; it is signed by the President und Registrar or by the Secretary acting as Registrar.

80. The Award is read out in public sitting, the agents and counsel of the parties being present or duly summoned to attend.

81. The Award, duly pronounced and notified to the agents of the parties, settles the dispute definitively and without appeal.

82. Any dispute arising between the parties as to the interpretation and execution of the Award shall, in the absence of an Agreement to the contrary, be submitted to the Tribunal which pronounced it.

83. The parties can reserve in the „Compromis" the right to demand the revision of the Award.

In this case and unless there be an Agreement to the contrary, the demand must be addressed to the Tribunal which pronounced the Award. It can only be made on the ground of the discovery of some new fact calculated to exercise a decisive influence upon the Award and which was unknown to the Tribunal and to the party which demanded the revision at the time the discussion was closed.

Proceedings for revision can only be instituted by a decision of the Tribunal expressly recording the existence of the new fact, recognizing in it the character described in the preceding paragraph, and declaring the demand admissible on this ground.

The „Compromis" fixes the period within which the demand for revision must be made.

84. The Award is not binding except on the parties in dispute.

When it concerns the interpretation of a Convention to which Powers other than those in dispute are parties, they shall inform all the Signatory Powers in good time. Each of these Powers is entitled to intervene in the case. If one or more avail themselves of this right, the interpretation contained in the Award is equally binding on them.

85. Each party pays its own expenses and an equal share of the expenses of the Tribunal.

CHAPTER IV.

Arbitration by Summary Procedure.

86. With a view to facilitating the working of the system of arbitration in disputes admitting of a summary procedure, the Contracting Powers adopt the following rules, which shall be observed in the absence of other arrangements and subject to the reservation that the provisions of Chapter III apply so far as may be.

87. Each of the parties in dispute appoints an Arbitrator. The two Arbitrators thus selected choose an Umpire. If they do not agree on this point, each of them proposes two candidates taken from the general list of the members of the Permanent Court exclusive of the members appointed by either of the parties and not being nationals of either of them; which of the candidates thus proposed shall be the Umpire is determined by lot.

The Umpire presides over the Tribunal, which gives its decisions by a majority of votes.

88. In the absence of any previous agreement the Tribunal, as soon as it is formed, settles the time within which the two parties must submit their respective cases to it.

89. Each party is represented before the Tribunal by an agent, who serves as intermediary between the Tribunal and the Government who appointed him.

90. The proceedings are conducted exclusively in writing. Each party, however, is entitled to ask that witnesses and experts should be called. The Tribunal has, for its part, the right to demand oral explanations from the agents of the two parties, as well as from the experts and witnesses whose appearance in Court it may consider useful.

PART V. — FINAL PROVISIONS.

91. The present Convention, duly ratified, shall replace, as between the Contracting Powers, the Convention for the Pacific Settlement of International Disputes of the 29th July, 1899.

92. The present Convention shall be ratified as soon as possible.

The ratifications shall be deposited at The Hague.

The first deposit of ratifications shall be recorded in a *procès-verbal* signed by the Representatives of the Powers which take part therein and by the Netherland Minister for Foreign Affairs.

The subsequent deposits of ratifications shall be made by means of a written notification, addressed to the Netherland Government and accompanied by the instrument of ratification.

A duly certified copy of the *procès-verbal* relative to the first deposit of ratifications, of the notifications mentioned in the preceding paragraph, and of the instruments of ratification, shall be immediately sent by the Netherland Government, through the diplomatic channel, to the Powers invited to the Second Peace Conference, as well as to those Powers which have adhered to the Convention. In the cases contemplated in the preceding paragraph, the said Government shall at the same time inform the Powers of the date on which it received the notification.

93. Non-Signatory Powers which have been invited to the Second Peace Conference may adhere to the present Convention.

The Power which desires to adhere notifies its intention in writing to the Netherland Government, forwarding to it the act of adhesion, which shall be deposited in the archives of the said Government.

This Government shall immediately forward to all the other Powers invited to the Second Peace Conference a duly certified copy of the notification as well as of the act of adhesion, mentioning the date on which it received the notification.

94. The conditions on which the Powers which have not been invited to the Second Peace Conference may adhere to the present Convention shall form the subject of a subsequent Agreement between the Contracting Powers.

95. The present Convention shall take effect, in the case of the Powers which were not a party to the first deposit of ratifications, sixty days after the date of the *procès-verbal* of this deposit, and, in the case of the Powers which ratify subsequently or which adhere, sixty days after the notification of their ratification or of their adhesion has been received by the Netherland Government.

96. In the event of one of the Contracting Parties wishing to denounce the present Convention, the denunciation shall be notified in writing to the Netherland Government, which shall immediately communicate a duly certified copy of the notification to all the other Powers informing them of the date on which it was received.

The denunciation shall only have effect in regard to the notifying Power, and one year after the notification has reached the Netherland Government.

97. A register kept by the Netherland Minister for Foreign Affairs shall give the date of the deposit of ratifications effected in virtue of Article 92, paragraphs 3 and 4, as well as the date on which the notifications of adhesion (Article 93, paragraph 2) or of denunciation (Article 96, paragraph 1) have been received.

Each Contracting Power is entitled to have access to this register and to be supplied with duly certified extracts from it.

VII. CONVENTION

RESPECTING THE LIMITATION OF THE EMPLOYMENT OF FORCE FOR THE RECOVERY OF CONTRACT DEBTS.

2d PEACE CONFERENCE, THE HAGUE, 18 OCT. 1907. II.

ART. 1. The Contracting Powers agree not to have recourse to armed force for the recovery of contract debts claimed from the Government of one country by the Government of another country as being due to its nationals.

This undertaking is, however, only applicable when the debtor State refuses or neglects to reply to an offer of arbitration, or, after accepting the offer, prevents any „Compromis" from being agreed on, or, after the arbitration, fails to submit to the award.

2. It is further agreed that the arbitration mentioned in paragraph 2 of the foregoing Article shall be subject to the procedure laid down in Part IV, Chapter III, of The Hague Convention for the Pacific Settlement of International Disputes. The award shall determine, except where otherwise agreed between the parties, the validity of the claim, the amount of the debt, and the time and mode of payment.

3. The present Convention shall be ratified as soon as possible.

The ratifications shall be deposited at The Hague.

The first deposit of ratifications shall be recorded in a *procès-verbal* signed by the Representatives of the Powers taking part therein and by the Netherland Minister for Foreign Affairs.

The subsequent deposits of ratifications shall be made by means of a written notification addressed to the Netherland Government and accompanied by the instrument of ratification.

A duly certified copy of the *procès-verbal* relative to the first deposit of ratifications, of the notifications mentioned in the preceding paragraph, as well as of the instruments of ratification, shall be sent immediately by the Netherland Government, through the diplomatic channel, to the Powers invited to the Second Peace Conference, as well as to the other Powers which have adhered to the Convention. In the cases contemplated in the preceding paragraph, the said Government shall inform them at the same time of the date on which it received the notification.

4. Non-Signatory Powers may adhere to the present Convention.

The Power which desires to adhere notifies its intention in writing to the Netherland Government, forwarding to it the act of adhesion, which shall be deposited in the archives of the said Government.

The said Government shall forward immediately to all the other Powers invited to the Second Peace Conference a duly certified copy of the notification, as well as of the act of adhesion, mentioning the date on which it received the notification.

5. The present Convention shall come into force, in the case of the Powers which were a party to the first deposit of ratifications, sixty days after the date of the *procès-verbal* of this deposit, in the case of the Powers which ratify subsequently or which adhere, sixty days after the notification of their ratification or of their adhesion has been received by the Netherland Government.

6. In the event of one of the Contracting Powers wishing to denounce the present Convention,the denunciation shall be notified in writing to the Netherland Government, which shall immediately communicate a duly certified copy of the notification to all the other Powers, informing them at the same time of date on which it was received.

The denunciation shall only have effect in regard to the notifying Power, and one year after the notification has reached the Netherland Government.

7. A register kept by the Netherland Ministry for Foreign Affairs shall give the date of the deposit of ratifications made in virtue of Article 3, paragraphs 3 and 4, as well as the date on which the notifications of adhesion (Article 4, paragraph 2) or of denunciation (Article 6, paragraph) 1) were received.

Each Contracting Power is entitled to have access to this register and to be supplied with duly certified extracts from it.

VIII. CONVENTION

RELATIVE TO THE OPENING OF HOSTILITIES.

2d PEACE CONFERENCE, THE HAGUE, 18 OCT. 1907. III.

ART. 1. The Contracting Powers recognize that hostilities between themselves must not commence without previous and explicit warning, in the form either of a reasoned declaration of war or of an ultimatum with conditional declaration of war.

2. The existence of a state of war must be notified to the neutral Powers without delay, and shall not take effect in regard to them until after the receipt of a notification, which may, however, be given by telegraph. Neutral Powers, nevertheless, cannot rely on the absence of notification if it is clearly established that they were in fact aware of the existence of a state of war.

3. Article 1 of the present Convention shall take effect in case of war between two or more of the Contracting Powers.

Article 2 is binding as between a belligerent Power which is a party to the Convention and neutral Powers which are also parties to the Convention.

Art. 4—8 = VII Art. 3—7.

IX. CONVENTION

CONCERNING THE LAWS AND CUSTOMS OF WAR ON LAND.

2d PEACE CONFERENCE, THE HAGUE, 18 OCT. 1907. IV.

ART. 1. The Contracting Powers shall issue instructions to their armed land forces which shall be in conformity with the Regulations respecting the Laws and Customs of War on Land, annexed to the present Convention.

2. The provisions contained in the Regulations referred to in Article 1, as well as in the present Convention, do not apply except between Contracting Powers, and then only if all the belligerents are parties to the Convention.

3. A belligerent party which violates the provisions of the said Regulations shall, if the case demands, be liable to pay compensation. It shall be responsible for all acts committed by persons forming part of its armed forces.

4. The present Convention, duly ratified, shall as between the Contracting Powers, be substituted for the Convention of the 29th July, 1899, respecting the Laws and Customs of War on Land.

The Convention of 1899 remains in force as between the Powers which signed it, and which do not also ratify the present Convention.

Art. 5—9 = VII Art. 3—7.

ANNEX TO THE CONVENTION.

REGULATIONS RESPECTING THE LAWS AND CUSTOMS OF WAR ON LAND.

SECTION I. — OF BELLIGERENTS.

CHAPTER I.

THE QUALIFICATIONS OF BELLIGERENTS.

ART. 1. The laws, rights, and duties of war apply not only to armies, but also to militia and volunteer corps fulfilling the following conditions:

1. To be commanded by a person responsible for his subordinates;
2. To have a fixed distinctive emblem recognizable at a distance;
3. To carry arms openly; and
4. To conduct their operations in accordance with the laws and customs of war.

In countries where militia or volunteer corps constitute the army, or form part of it, they are included under the denomination „army."

2. The inhabitants of a territory which has not been occupied, who, on the approach of the enemy, spontaneously take up arms to resist the invading troops without having had time to organize themselves in accordance with Article 1, shall be regarded as belligerents if they carry arms openly and if they respect the laws and customs of war.

3. The armed forces of the belligerent parties may consist of combatants and non-combatants. In the case of capture by the enemy, both have a right to be treated as prisoners of war.

CHAPTER II.

Prisoners of War.

4. Prisoners of war are in the power of the hostile Government, but not of the individuals or corps who capture them.

They must be humanely treated.

All their personal belongings, except arms, horses, and military papers, remain their property.

5. Prisoners of war may be interned in a town, fortress, camp, or other place, and bound not to go beyond certain fixed limits; but they cannot be confined except as an indispensable measure of safety and only while the circumstances which necessitate the measure continue to exist.

6. The State may utilize the labour of prisoners of war according to their rank and aptitude, officers excepted. The tasks shall not be excessive and shall have no connection with the operations of the war.

Prisoners may be authorized to work for the public service, for private persons, or on their own account.

Work done for the State is paid at the rates in force for work of a similar kind done by soldiers of the national army, or, if there are none in force, at a rate according to the work executed.

When the work is for other branches of the public service or for private persons the conditions are settled in agreement with the military authorities.

The wages of the prisoners shall go towards improving their position, and the balance shall be paid them on their release, after deducting the cost of their maintenance.

7. The Government into whose hands prisoners of war have fallen is charged with their maintenance.

In the absence of a special agreement between the belligerents, prisoners of war shall be treated as regards board, lodging, and clothing on the same footing as the troops of the Government who captured them.

8. Prisoners of war shall be subject to the laws, regulations, and orders in force in the army of the State in whose power they are. Any act of insubordination justifies the adoption towards them of such measures of severity as may be considered necessary.

Escaped prisoners who are retaken before being able to rejoin their own army or before leaving the territory occupied by the army which captured them are liable to disciplinary punishment.

Prisoners who, after succeeding in escaping, are again taken prisoners, are not liable to any punishment on account of the previous flight.

9. Every prisoner of war is bound to give, if he is questioned on the subject, his true name and rank, and if he infringes this rule, he is liable to have the advantages given to prisoners of his class curtailed.

10. Prisoners of war may be set at liberty on parole if the laws of their country allow, and, in such cases, they are bound, on their personal honour, scrupulously to fulfil, both towards their own Government and the Government by whom they were made prisoners, the engagements they have contracted.

In such cases their own Government is bound neither to require of nor accept from them any service incompatible with the parole given.

11. A prisoner of war cannot be compelled to accept his liberty on parole; similarly the hostile Government is not obliged to accede to the request of the prisoner to be set at liberty on parole.

12. Prisoners of war liberated on parole and recaptured bearing arms against the Government to whom they had pledged their honour, or against the allies of that Government, forfeit their right to be treated as prisoners of war, and can be brought before the Courts.

13. Individuals who follow an army without directly belonging to it, such as newspaper correspondents and reporters, sutlers and contractors, who fall into the enemy's hands and whom the latter thinks expedient to detain, are entitled to be treated as prisoners of war, provided they are in possession of a certificate from the military authorities of the army which they were accompanying.

14. An inquiry office for prisoners of war is instituted on the commencement of hostilities in each of the belligerent States, and, when necessary, in neutral countries which have received belligerents in their territory. It is the function of this office to reply to all inquiries about the prisoners. It receives from the various services concerned full information respecting internments and transfers, releases on parole, exchanges, escapes, admissions into hospital, deaths, as well as other information necessary to enable it to make out and keep up to date an individual return for each prisoner of war. The office must state in this return the regimental number, name and surname, age, place of origin, rank, unit, wounds, date and place of capture, internment, wounding, and death, as well as any observations of a special character. The individual return shall be sent to the Government of the other belligerent after the conclusion of peace.

It is likewise the function of the inquiry office to receive and collect all objects of personal use, valuables, letters, &c., found on the field of battle or left by prisoners who have been released on parole, or exchanged, or who have escaped, or died in hospitals or ambulances, and to forward them to those concerned.

15. Relief societies for prisoners of war, which are properly constituted in accordance with the laws of their country and with the object of serving as the channel for charitable effort shall receive from the belligerents, for themselves and their duly accredited agents every facility for the efficient performance of their humane task within the bounds imposed by military necessities and administrative regulations. Agents of these societies may be admitted to the places of internment for the purpose of distributing relief, as also to the halting places of repatriated prisoners, if furnished with a personal permit by the military authorities, and on giving an undertaking in writing to comply with all measures of order and police which the latter may issue.

16. Inquiry offices enjoy the privilege of free postage. Letters, money orders, and valuables, as well as parcels by post, intended for prisoners of war, or dispatched by them, shall be exempt from all postal duties in the countries of origin and destination, as well as in the countries they pass through.

Presents and relief in kind for prisoners of war shall be admitted free of all import or other duties, as well as of payments for carriage by the State railways.

17. Officers taken prisoners shall receive the same rate of pay as officers of corresponding rank in the country where they are detained, the amount to be ultimately refunded by their own Government.

18. Prisoners of war shall enjoy complete liberty in the exercise of their religion, including attendance at the services of whatever Church they may belong to, on the sole condition that they comply with the measures of order and police issued by the military authorities.

19. The wills of prisoners of war are received or drawn up in the same way as for soldiers, of the national army.

The same rules shall be observed regarding death certificates as well as for the burial of prisoners of war, due regard being paid to their grade and rank.

20. After the conclusion of peace, the repatriation of prisoners of war shall be carried out as quickly as possible.

CHAPTER III.

The Sick and Wounded.

21. The obligations of belligerents with regard to the sick and wounded are governed by the Geneva Convention.

SECTION II. — HOSTILITIES.

CHAPTER I.

Means of Injuring the Enemy, Sieges, and Bombardments.

22. The right of belligerents to adopt means of injuring the enemy is not unlimited.

23. In addition to the prohibitions provided by special Conventions, it is especially forbidden:

a. To employ poison or poisoned weapons;
b. To kill or wound treacherously individuals belonging to the hostile nation or army;
c. To kill or wound an enemy who, having laid down his arms, or having no longer means of defence, has surrendered at discretion;
d. To declare that no quarter will be given;
e. To employ arms, projectiles, or material calculated to cause unnecessary suffering;
f. To make improper use of a flag of truce, of the national flag, or of the military insignia and uniform of the enemy, as well as the distinctive badges of the Geneva Convention;
g. To destroy or seize the enemy's property, unless such destruction or seizure be imperatively demanded by the necessities of war;
h. To declare abolished, suspended, or inadmissible in a Court of law the rights and actions of the nationals of the hostile party.

A belligerent is likewise forbidden to compel the nationals of the hostile party to take part in the operations of war directed against their own country, even if they were in the belligerent's service before the commencement of the war.

24. Ruses of war and the employment of measures necessary for obtaining information about the enemy and the country are considered permissible.

25. The attack or bombardment, by whatever means, of towns, villages, dwellings, or buildings which are undefended is prohibited.

26. The officer in command of an attacking force must, before commencing a bombardment, except in cases of assault, do all in his power to warn the authorities.

27. In sieges and bombardments all necessary steps must be taken to spare, as far as possible, buildings dedicated to religion, art, science, or charitable purposes, historic monuments, hospitals, and places where the sick and wounded are collected, provided they are not being used at the time for military purposes.

It is the duty of the besieged to indicate the presence of such buildings or places by distinctive and visible signs, which shall be notified to the enemy beforehand.

28. The pillage of a town or place, even when taken by assault, is prohibited.

CHAPTER II.

Spies.

29. A person can only be considered a spy when, acting clandestinely or on false pretences, he obtains or endeavours to obtain information in the zone of operations of a belligerent, with the intention of communicating it to the hostile party.

Thus, soldiers not wearing a disguise who have penetrated into the zone of operations of the hostile army ,for the purpose of obtaining information, are not considered spies. Similarly, the following are not considered spies: Soldiers and civilians, carrying out their mission openly, intrusted with the delivery of despatches intended either for their own army or for the enemy's army. To this class belong likewise persons sent in balloons for the purpose of carrying despatches and, generally, of maintaining communications between the different parts of an army or a territory.

30. A spy taken in the act shall not be punished without previous trial.

31. A spy who, after rejoining the army to which he belongs, is subsequently captured by the enemy, is treated as a prisoner of war, and incurs no responsibility for his previous acts of espionage.

CHAPTER III.

Flags of Truce.

32. A person is regarded as bearing a flag, of truce who has been authorized by one of the belligerents to enter into communication with the other, and who advances bearing a white flag. He has a right to inviolability, as well as the trumpeter, bugler or drummer, the flag-bearer and interpreter who may accompany him.

33. The commander to whom a flag of truce is sent is not in all cases obliged to receive it.

He may take all the necessary steps to prevent the envoy taking advantage of his mission to obtain information.

In case of abuse, he has the right to detain the envoy temporarily.

34. The envoy loses his rights of inviolability if it is proved in a clear and incontestable manner that he has taken advantage of his privileged position to provoke or commit an act of treachery.

CHAPTER IV.

Capitulations.

35. Capitulations agreed upon between the contracting parties must take into account the rules of military honour.

Once settled, they must be scrupulously observed by both parties.

CHAPTER V.

Armistices.

36. An armistice suspends military operations by mutual agreement between the belligerent parties. If its duration is not defined, the belligerent parties may resume operations at any time, provided always that the enemy is warned within the time agreed upon, in accordance with the terms of the armistice.

37. An armistice may be general or local. The first suspends the military operations of the belligerent States everywhere; the second only between certain fractions of the belligerent armies and within a fixed radius.

38. An armistice must be notified officially and in good time to the competent authorities and to the troops. Hostilities are suspended immediately after the notification, or on the date fixed.

39. It rests with the contracting parties to settle, in the terms of the armistice, what communications may be held in the theatre of war with the inhabitants and between the inhabitants of one belligerent State and those of the other.

40. Any serious violation of the armistice by one of the parties gives the other party the right of denouncing it, and even, in cases of urgency, of recommencing hostilities immediately.

41. A violatin of the terms of the armistice by private persons acting on their own initiative only entitles the injured party to demand the punishment of the offenders or, if necessary, compensation for the losses sustained.

SECTION III. — MILITARY AUTHORITY OVER THE TERRITORY OF THE HOSTILE STATE.

42. Territory is considered occupied when it is actually placed under the authority of the hostile army.

The occupation extends only to the territory where such authority has been established and can be exercised.

43. The authority of the legitimate power having in fact passed into the hands of the occupant, the latter shall take all the measures in his power to restore, and ensure, as far as possible, public order and safety, while respecting, unless absolutely prevented, the laws in force in the country.

44. A belligerent is forbidden to force the inhabitants of territory occupied by it to furnish information about the army of the other belligerent, or about its means of defence.

45. It is forbidden to compel the inhabitants of occupied territory to swear allegiance to the hostile Power.

46. Family honour and rights, the lives of persons, and private property, as well as religious convictions and practice, must be respected.

Private property cannot be confiscated.

47. Pillage is formally forbidden.

48. If, in the territory occupied, the occupant collects the taxes, dues, and tolls imposed for the benefit of the State, he shall do so, as far as is possible, in accordance with the rules of assessment and incidence in force, and shall in consequence be bound to defray the expenses of the administration of the occupied territory to the same extent as the legitimate Government was so bound.

49. If, in addition to the taxes mentioned in the above Article, the occupant levies other money contributions in the occupied territory, this shall only be for the needs of the army or of the administration of the territory in question.

50. No general penalty, pecuniary or otherwise, shall be inflicted upon the population on account of the acts of individuals for which they cannot be regarded as jointly and severally responsible.

51. No contribution shall be collected except under a written order and on the responsibility of a Commander-in-chief.

The collection of the said contribution shall only be effected as far as possible in accordance with the rules of assessment and incidence of the taxes in force.

For every contribution a receipt shall be given to the contributors.

52. Requisitions in kind and services shall not be demanded from municipalities or inhabitants except for the needs of the army of occupation. They shall be in proportion to the resources of the country, and of such a nature as not to involve the inhabitants in the obligation of taking part in military operations against their own country.

Such requisitions and services shall only be demanded on the authority of the commander in the locality occupied.

Contributions in kind shall as far as possible be paid for in cash; if not, a receipt shall be given and the payment of the amount due shall be made as soon as possible.

53. An army of occupation can only take possession of cash, funds, and realizable securities which are strictly the property of the State, depôts of arms, means of transport, stores and supplies, and, generally, all movable property belonging to the State which may be used for military operations.

All appliances, whether on land, at sea, or in the air, adapted for the transmission of news, or for the transport of persons or things, exclusive of cases governed by naval law, depôts of arms, and, generally, all kinds of ammunition of war, may be seized, even if they belong to private individuals, but must be restored and compensation fixed when peace is made.

54. Submarine cables connecting an occupied territory with a neutral territory shall not be seized or destroyed except in the case of absolute necessity. They must likewise be restored and compensation fixed when peace is made.

55. The occupying State shall be regarded only as administrator and usufructuary of public buildings, real estate, forests, and agricultural estates belonging to the hostile State, and situated in the occupied country. It must safeguard the capital of these properties, and administer them in accordance with the rules of usufruct.

56. The property of municipalities, that of institutions dedicated to religion, charity and education, the arts and sciences, even when State property, shall be treated as private property.

All seizure of, destruction or wilful damage done to institutions of this character, historic monuments, works of art and science, is forbidden, and should be made the subject of legal proceedings.

X. CONVENTION

RESPECTING THE RIGHTS AND DUTIES OF NEUTRAL POWERS AND PERSONS IN WAR ON LAND.

2d PEACE CONFERENCE, THE HAGUE, 18 OCT. 1907. V.

CHAPTER I.

THE RIGHTS AND DUTIES OF NEUTRAL POWERS.

ART. 1. The territory of neutral Powers is inviolable.

2. Belligerents are forbidden to move troops or convoys of either munitions of war or supplies across the territory of a neutral Power.

3. Belligerents are likewise forbidden to:

a. Erect on the territory of a neutral Power a wireless telegraphy station or other apparatus for the purpose of communicating with belligerent forces on land or sea;

b. Use any installation of this kind established by them before the war on the territory of a neutral Power for purely military purposes, and which has not been opened for the service of public messages.

4. Corps of combatants cannot be formed nor recruiting agencies opened on the territory of a neutral Power to assist the belligerents.

5. A neutral Power must not allow any of the acts referred to in Articles 2 to 4 to occur on its territory.

It is not called upon to punish acts in violation of its neutrality unless the said acts have been committed on its own territory.

6. The responsibility of a neutral Power is not engaged by the fact of persons crossing the frontier separating to offer their services to one of the belligerents.

7. A neutral Power is not called upon to prevent the export or transport, on behalf of one or other of the belligerents, of arms, munitions of war, or, in general, of anything which can be of use to an army or a fleet.

8. A neutral Power is not called upon to forbid or restrict the use on behalf of the belligerents of telegraph or telephone cables or of wireless telegraphy apparatus belonging to it or to Companies or private individuals.

9. Every measure of restriction or prohibition taken by a neutral Power in regard to the matters referred to in Articles 7 and 8 must be impartially applied by it to both belligerents.

A neutral Power must see to the same obligation being observed by Companies or private individuals owning telegraph or telephone cables or wireless telegraphy apparatus.

10. The fact of a neutral Power resisting, even by force, attempts to violate its neutrality cannot be regarded as a hostile act.

CHAPTER II.

Belligerents Interned and Wounded tended in Neutral Territory.

11. A neutral Power which receives on its territory troops belonging to the belligerent armies shall intern them, as far as possible, at a distance from the theatre of war.

It may keep them in camps and even confine them in fortresses or in places set apart for this purpose.

It shall decide whether officers can be left at liberty on giving their parole not to leave the neutral territory without permission.

12. In the absence of a special Convention to the contrary, the neutral Power shall supply the interned with the food, clothing, and relief required by humanity.

At the conclusion of peace the expenses caused by the internment shall be made good.

13. A neutral Power which receives escaped prisoners of war shall leave them at liberty. If it allows them to remain in its territory it may assign them a place of residence.

The same rule applies to prisoners of war brought by troops taking refuge in the territory of a neutral Power.

14. A neutral Power may authorize the passage into its territory of the sick and wounded belonging to the belligerent armies, on condition that the trains bringing them shall carry neither personnel or war material. In such a case, the neutral Power is bound to take whatever measures of safety and control are necessary for the purpose.

The sick or wounded brought under these conditions into neutral territory by one of the belligerents, and belonging to the hostile party, must be guarded by the neutral Power so as to ensure their not taking part again in the military operations. The same duty shall devolve on the neutral State with regard to wounded or sick of the other army who may be committed to its care.

15. The Geneva Convention applies to sick and wounded interned in neutral territory.

CHAPTER III.

Neutral Persons.

16. The nationals of a State which is not taking part in the war are considered as neutrals.

17. A neutral cannot avail himself of his neutrality:

a. If he commits hostile acts against a belligerent;

b. It he commits acts in favour of a belligerent, particulary if he voluntarily enlists in the ranks of the armed force of one of the parties.

In such a case, the neutral shall not be more severely treated by the belligerent as against whom he has abandoned his neutrality than a national of the other belligerent State could be for the same act.

18. The following acts shall not be considered as committed in favour of one belligerent in the sense of Article 17, letter *b*:

a. Supplies furnished or loans made to one of the belligerents, provided that the person who furnishes the supplies or who makes the loans lives neither in the territory of the other party nor in the territory occupied by him, and that the supplies do not come from these territories;

b. Services rendered in matters of police or civil administration.

CHAPTER IV.

Railway Material.

19. Railway material coming from the territory of neutral Powers, whether it be the property of the said Powers or of Companies or private persons, and recognizable as such, shall not be requisitioned or utilized by a belligerent except where and to the extent that it is absolutely necessary, It shall be sent back as soon as possible to the country of origin.

A neutral Power may likewise, in case of necessity, retain and utilize to an equal extent material coming from the territory of the belligerent Power.

Compensation shall be paid by one party or the other in proportion to the material used, and to the period of usage.

CHAPTER V.

Final Provisions.

20. The provisions of the present Convention do not apply except between Contracting Powers, and then only if all the belligerents are parties to the Convention.

Art. 21—25 = VII Art. 3—7.

XI. CONVENTION

RELATIVE TO THE STATUS OF ENEMY MERCHANT-SHIPS AT THE OUTBREAK OF HOSTILITIES.

2d PEACE CONFERENCE, THE HAGUE, 18 OCT. 1907. VI.

ART. 1. When a merchant-ship belonging to one of the belligerent Powers is at the commencement of hostilities in an enemy port, it is desirable that it should be allowed to depart freely, either immediately, or after a reasonable number of days of grace, and to proceed, after being furnished with a pass, direct to its port of destination or any other port indicated.

The same rule should apply in the case of a ship which has left its last port of departure before the commencement of the war and entered a port belonging to the enemy while still ignorant that hostilities had broken out.

2. A merchant-ship unable, owing to circumstances of *force majeure*, to leave the enemy port within the period contemplated in the above Article, or which was not allowed to leave, cannot be confiscated.

The belligerent may only detain it, without payment of compensation, but subject to the obligation of restoring it after the war, or requisition it on payment of compensation.

3. Enemy merchant-ships which left their last port of departure before the commencement of the war, and are encountered on the high seas while still ignorant of the outbreak of hostilities cannot be confiscated. They are only liable to detention on the understanding that they shall be restored after the war without compensation, or to be requisitioned, or even destroyed, on payment of compensation, but in such case provision must be made for the safety of the persons on board as well as the security of the ship's papers.

After touching at a port in their own country or at a neutral port, these ships are subject to the laws and customs of maritime war.

4. Enemy cargo on board the vessels referred to in Articles 1 and 2 is likewise liable to be detained and restored after the termination of the war without payment of compensation, or to be requisitioned on payment of compensation, with or without the ship.

The same rule applies in the case of cargo on board the vessels referred to in Article 3.

5. The present Convention does not affect merchant-ships whose build shows that they are intended for conversion into war-ships.

6. The provisions of the present Convention do not apply except between Contracting Powers, and then only if all the belligerents are parties to the Convention.

Art. 7—11 = VII Art. 3—7.

XII. CONVENTION

RELATIVE TO THE CONVERSION OF MERCHANT-SHIPS INTO WAR-SHIPS.

2d PEACE CONFERENCE, THE HAGUE, 18 OCT. 1907. VII.

ART. 1. A merchant-ship converted into a war-ship cannot have the rights and duties accruing to such vessels unless it is placed under the direct authority, immediate control, and responsibility of the Power whose flag it flies.

2. Merchant-ships converted into war-ships must bear the external marks which distinguish the war-ships of their nationality.

3. The commander must be in the service of the State and duly commissioned by the competent authorities. His name must figure on the list of the officers of the fighting fleet.

4. The crew must be subject to military discipline.

5. Every merchant-ship converted into a war-ship must observe in its operations the laws and customs of war.

6. A belligerent who converts a merchant-ship into a war-ship must, as soon as possible, announce such conversion in the list of war-ships.

7. The provisions of the present Convention do not apply except between Contracting Powers, and then only if all the belligerents are parties to the Convention.

Art. 8—12 = VII Art. 3—7.

XIII. CONVENTION

RELATIVE TO THE LAYING OF AUTOMATIC SUBMARINE CONTACT MINES.

2d PEACE CONFERENCE, THE HAGUE, 18 OCT. 1907. VIII.

ART. 1. It is forbidden:

1. To lay unanchored automatic contact mines, except when they are so constructed as to become harmless one hour at most after the person who laid them ceases to control them;
2. To lay anchored automatic contact mines which do not become harmless as soon as they have broken loose from their moorings;
3. To use torpedoes which do not become harmless when they have missed their mark.

2. It is forbidden to lay automatic contact mines off the coast and ports of the enemy, with the sole object of intercepting commercial shipping.

3. When anchored automatic contact mines are employed, every possible precaution must be taken for the security of peaceful shipping.

The belligerents undertake to do their utmost to render these mines harmless within a limited time, and, should they cease to be under surveillance, to notify the danger zones as soon as military exigencies permit, by a notice addressed to shipowners, which must also be communicated to the Governments through the diplomatic channel.

4. Neutral Powers which lay automatic contact mines off their coasts must observe the same rules and take the same precautions as are imposed on belligerents.

The neutral Power must inform ship-owners, by a notice issured in advance, where automatic contact mines have been laid. This notice must be communicated at once to the Governments through the diplomatic channel.

5. At the close of the war, the Contracting Powers undertake to do their utmost to remove the mines which they have laid, each Power removing its own mines.

As regards anchored automatic contact mines laid by one of the belligerents off the coast of the other, their position must be notified to the other party by the Power which laid them, and each Power must proceed with the least possible delay to remove the mines in its own waters.

6. The Contracting Powers which do not at present own perfected mines of the pattern contemplated in the present Convention, and which, consequently, could not at present carry out the rules laid down in Articles 1 and 3, undertake to convert the *matériel* of their mines as soon as possible, so as to bring it into conformity with the foregoing requirements.

7. The provisions of the present Convention do not apply except between Contracting Powers, and then only if all the belligerents are parties to the Convention.

8. The present Convention shall be ratified as soon as possible.

The ratifications shall be deposited at The Hague.

The first deposit of ratifications shall be recorded in a *procès-verbal* signed by the Representatives of the Powers which take part therein and by the Netherland Minister for Foreign Affairs.

The subsequent deposits of ratifications shall be made by means of a written notification addressed to the Netherland Government and accompanied by the instrument of ratification.

A duly certified copy of the *procès-verbal* relative to the first deposit of ratifications, of the notifications mentioned in the preceding paragraph, as wel as of the instruments of ratification,shall be at once sent, by the Netherland Government, through the diplomatic channel,to the Powers invited to the Second Peace Conference, as well as to the other Powers which have adhered to the Convention. In the cases contemplated in the preceding paragraph, the said Government shall inform them at the same time of the date on which it has received the notification.

9. Non-Signatory Powers may adhere to the present Convention.

The Power which desires to adhere notifies in writing its intention to the Netherland Government, transmitting to it the act of adhesion, which shall be deposited in the archives of the said Government.

This Government shall at once transmit to all the other Powers a duly certified copy of the notification as well as of the act of adhesion, stating the date on which it received the notification.

10. The present Convention shall come into force, in the case of the Powers which were a party to the first deposit of ratifications, sixty days after the date of the *procès-verbal* of this deposit, and, in the case of the Powers which ratify subsequently or adhere, sixty days after the notification of their ratification or of their adhesion has been received by the Netherland Government.

11. The present Convention shall remain in force for seven years, dating from the sixtieth day after the date of the first deposit of ratifications.

Unless denounced, it shall continue in force after the expiration of this period.

The denunciation shall be notified in writing to the Netherland Government, which shall at once communicate a duly certified copy of the notification to all the Powers, informing them of the date on which it was received.

The denunciation shall only have effect in regard to the notifying Power, and six months after the notification has reached the Netherland Government.

12. The Contracting Powers undertake to reopen the question of the employment of automatic contact mines six months before the expiration of the period contemplated in the first paragraph of the preceding Article, in the event of the question not having been already reopened and settled by the Third Peace Conference.

If the Contracting Powers conclude a fresh Convention relative to the employment of mines, the present Convention shall cease to be applicable from the moment it comes into force.

13. A register kept by the Netherland Ministry for Foreign Affairs shall give the date of the deposit of ratifications made in virtue of Article 8, paragraphs 3 and 4, as well as the date on which the notifications of adhesion (Article 9, paragraph 2) or of denunciation (Article 9, paragraph 3) have been received.

Each Contracting Power is entitled to have access to this register and to be supplied with duly certified extracts from it.

XIV. CONVENTION

RESPECTING BOMBARDMENTS BY NAVAL FORCES IN TIME OF WAR.

2d PEACE CONFERENCE, THE HAGUE, 18 OCT. 1907. IX.

CHAPTER I.

The Bombardment of Undefended Ports, Towns, Villages, Dwellings, or Buildings.

Art. 1. The bombardment by naval forces of undefended ports, towns, villages, dwellings, or buildings is forbidden.

A place cannot be bombarded solely because automatic submarine contact mines are anchored off the harbour.

2. Military works, military or naval establishments, depôts of arms or *warmatériel*, workshops or plant which could be utilized for the needs of the hostile fleet or army, and the ships of war in the harbour, are not, however, included in this prohibition. The commander of a naval force may destroy them with artillery, after a summons followed by a reasonable time of waiting, if all other means are impossible, and when the local authorities have not themselves destroyed them within the time fixed.

He incurs no responsibility for any unavoidable damage which may be caused by a bombardment under such circumstances.

If for military reasons immediate action is necessary, and no delay can be allowed the enemy, it is understood that the prohibition to bombard the undefended town holds good, as in the case given in paragraph 1, and that the commander shall take all due measures in order that the town may suffer as little harm as possible.

3. After due notice has been given, the bombardment of undefended ports, towns, villages, dwellings, or buildings may be commenced, it the local authorities, after a formal summons has been made to them, decline to comply with requisitions for provisions or supplies necessary for the immediate use of the naval force before the place in question.

These requisitions shall be in proportion to the resources of the place. They shall only be demanded in the name of the commander of the said naval force, and they shall, as far as possible, be paid for in cash; if not, they shall be evidenced by receipts.

4. Undefended ports, towns, villages, dwellings, or buildings may not be bombarded on account of failure to pay money contributions.

CHAPTER II.

General Provisions.

5. In bombardments by naval forces all the necessary measures must be taken by the commander to spare as far as possible sacred edifices, buildings used for artistic, scientific, or charitable purposes, historic monuments, hospitals, and places where the sick or wounded are collected, on the understanding that they are not used at the same time for military purposes.

It is the duty of the inhabitants to indicate such monuments, edifices, or places by visible signs, which shall consist of large stiff rectangular panels divided diagonally into two coloured triangular portions, the upper portion black, the lower portion white.

6. If the military situation permits, the commander of the attacking naval force, before commencing the bombardment, must do his utmost to warn the authorities.

7. A town or place, even when taken by storm, may not be pillaged.

CHAPTER III.

Final Provisions.

8. The provisions of the present Convention do not apply except between Contracting Powers, and then only if all the belligerents are parties to the Convention.

Art. 9—13 = VII Art. 3—7.

XV. CONVENTION

FOR THE ADAPTATION OF THE PRINCIPLES OF THE GENEVA CONVENTION TO MARITIME WARFARE.

2d PEACE CONFERENCE, THE HAGUE, 18 OCT. 1907. X.

ART. 1. Military hospital-ships, that is to say, ships constructed or assigned by States specially and solely with a view to assisting the wounded, sick, and shipwrecked, the names of which have been communicated to the belligerent Powers at the commencement or during the course of hostilities, and in any case before they are employed, shall be respected, and cannot be captured while hostilities last.

These ships, moreover, are not on the same footing as war-ships as regards their stay in a neutral port.

2. Hospital-ships, equipped wholly or in part at the expense of private individuals or officially recognized relief societies, shall be likewise respected and exempt from capture, if the belligerent Power to whom they belong has given them an official commission and has notified their names to the hostile Power at the commencement of or during hostilities, and in any case before they are employed.

These ships must be provided with a certificate from the competent authorities declaring that the vessels have been under their control while fitting out and on final departure.

3. Hospital-ships, equipped wholly or in part at the expense of private individuals or officially recognized societies of neutral countries, shall be respected and exempt from capture, on condition that they are placed under the control of one of the belligerents, with the previous, consent of their own Government and with the authorization of the belligerent himself, and that the latter has notified their name to his adversary af the commencement of or during hostilities, and in any case, before they are employed.

4. The ships mentioned in Articles 1, 2, and 3 shall afford relief and assistance to the wounded, sick, and shipwrecked of the belligerents without distinction of nationality.

The Governments undertake not to use these ships for any military purpose.

These vessels must in no wise hamper the movements of the combatants.

During and after an engagement they will act at their own risk and peril.

The belligerents shall have the right to control and search them; they can refuse to help them, order them off, make them take a certain course, and put a Commissioner on board; they can even detain them, if important circumstances require it.

As far as possible, the belligerents shall enter in the log of the hospital-ships the orders which they give them.

5. Military hospital-ships shall be distinguished by being painted white outside with a horizontal band of green about a metre and a half in breadth.

The ships mentioned in Articles 2 and 3 shall be distinguished by being painted white outside with a horizontal band of red about a metre and a half in breadth.

The boats of the ships above mentioned, as also small craft which may be used for hospital work, shall be distinguished by similar painting.

All hospital-ships shall make themselves known by hoisting, with their national flag, the white flag with a red cross provided by the Geneva Convention, and further, if they belong to a neutral State, by flying at the mainmast the national flag of the belligerent under whose control they are placed.

Hospital-ships which, in the terms of Article 4, are detained by the enemy, must haul down the national flag of the belligerent to whom they belong.

The ships and boats above mentioned which wish to ensure by night the freedom from interference to which they are entitled, must, subject to the assent of the belligerent they are accompanying, take the necessary measures to render their special painting sufficiently plain.

6. The distinguishing signs referred to in Article 5 can only be used, whether in time of peace or war, for protecting or indicating the ships therein mentioned.

7. In the case of a fight on board a war-ship, the sick-wards shall be respected and spared as far as possible.

The said sick-wards and the *matériel* belonging to them remain subject to the laws of war; they cannot, however, be used for any purpose other than that for which they were originally intended, so long as they are required for the sick and wounded.

The commander, however, into whose power they have fallen may apply them to other purposes, if the military situation requires it, after seeing that the sick and wounded on board are properly provided for.

8. Hospital-ships and sick-wards of vessels are no longer entitled to protection if they are employed for the purpose of injuring the enemy.

The fact of the staff of the said ships and sick-wards being armed for maintaining order and for defending the sick and wounded, and the presence of wireless telegraphy apparatus on board, is not a sufficient reason for withdrawing protection.

9. Belligerents may appeal to the charity of the commanders of neutral merchant-ships, yachts, or boats to take on board and tend the sick and wounded.

Vessels responding to this appeal, and also vessels which have of their own accord rescued sick, wounded, or shipwrecked men, shall enjoy special protection and certain immunities. In no case can they be captured for having such persons on board, but, apart from special undertakings that have been made to them, they remain liable to capture for any violations of neutrality they may have committed.

10. The religious, medical, and hospital staff of any captured ship is inviolable, and its members cannot be made prisoners of war. On leaving the ship they take away with them the objects and surgical instruments which are their own private property.

This staff shall continue to discharge its duties while necessary, and can afterwards leave, when the Commander-in-chief considers it possible.

The belligerents must guarantee to the said staff, when it has fallen into their hands, the same allowances and pay which are given to the staff of corresponding rank in their own navy.

11. Sailors and soldiers on board, when sick or wounded, as well as other persons officially attached to fleets or armies, whatever their nationality, shall be respected and tended by the captors.

12. Any war-ship belonging to a belligerent may demand that sick, wounded, or shipwrecked men on board military hospital-ships, hospital-ships belonging to relief societies or to private individuals, merchant-ships, yachts, or boats, whatever the nationality of these vessels, should be handed over.

13. If sick, wounded, or shipwrecked persons are taken on board a neutral war-ship, every possible, precaution must be taken that they do not again take part in the operations of the war.

14. The shipwrecked, wounded, or sick of one of the belligerents who fall into the power of the other belligerent are prisoners of war. The captor must decide, according to circumstances, whether to keep them, send them to a port of his own country, to a neutral port, or even to an enemy port. In this last case, prisoners thus repatriated cannot serve again while the war lasts.

15. The shipwrecked, sick, or wounded, who are landed at a neutral port with the consent of the local authorities, must, unless an arrangement is made to the contrary between the neutral State and the belligerent States, be guarded by the neutral State so as to prevent them again taking part in the operations of the war.

The expenses of tending them in hospital and interning them shall be borne by the State to which the shipwrecked, sick, or wounded persons belong.

16. After every engagement, the two belligerents, so far as military interests permit, shall take steps to look for the shipwrecked, sick, and wounded, and to protect them, as well as the dead, against pillage and ill-treatment.

They shall see that the burial, whether by land or sea, or cremation of the dead shall be preceded by a careful examination of the corpse.

17. Each belligerent shall send, as early as possible, to the authorities of their country, navy, or army the military marks or documents of identity found on the dead and the description of the sick and wounded picked up by him.

The belligerents shall keep each other informed as to internments and transfers as well as to the admissions into hospital and deaths which have occurred among the sick and wounded in their hands. They shall collect all the objects of personal use, valuables, letters, &c., which are found in the captured ships, or which have been left by the sick or wounded who died in hospital, in order to have them forwarded to the persons concerned by the authorities of their own country.

18. The provisions of the present Convention do not apply except between Contracting Powers, and then only if all the belligerents are parties to the Convention.

19. The Commanders-in-chief of the belligerent fleets must see that the above Articles are properly carried out; they will have also to see to cases not covered thereby, in accordance with the instructions of their respective Governments and in conformity with the general principles of the present Convention.

20. The Signatory Powers shall take the necessary measures for bringing the provisions of the present Convention to the knowledge of their naval forces, and especially of the members entitled thereunder to immunity, and for making them known to the public.

21. The Signatory Powers likewise undertake to enact or to propose to their Legislatures, if their criminal laws are inadequate, the measures necessary for checking in time of war individual acts of pillage and ill-treatment in respect to the sick and wounded in the fleet, as well as for punishing, as an unjustifiable adoption of naval or military marks, the unauthorized use of the distinctive marks mentioned in Article 5 by vessels not protected by the present Convention.

They will communicate to each other, through the Netherland Government, the enactments for preventing such acts at the latest within five years of the ratification of the present Convention.

22. In the case of operations of war between the land and sea forces of belligerents, the provisions of the present Convention do not apply except between the forces actually on board ship.

23. The present Convention shall be ratified as soon as possible.

The ratifications shall be deposited at The Hague.

The first deposit of ratifications shall be recorded in a *procès-verbal* signed by the Representatives of the Powers taking part therein and by the Netherland Minister for Foreign Affairs.

Subsequent deposits of ratifications shall be made by means of a written notification addressed to the Netherland Government and accompanied by the instrument of ratification.

A certified copy of the *procès-verbal* relative to the first deposit of ratifications, of the notifications mentioned in the preceding paragraph, as well as of the instruments of ratification, shall be at once sent by the Netherland Government through the diplomatic channel to the Powers invited to the Second Peace Conference, as well as to the other Powers which have adhered to the Convention. In the cases contemplated in the preceding paragraph the said Government shall inform them at the same time of the date on which it received the notification.

24. Non-Signatory Powers which have accepted the Geneva Convention of the 6th July, 1906, may adhere to the present Convention.

The Power which desires to adhere notifies its intention to the Netherland Government in writing, forwarding to it the act of adhesion, which shall be deposited in the archives of the said Government.

The said Government shall at once transmit to all the other Powers a duly certified copy of the notification as well as of the act of adhesion, mentioning the date on which it received the notification.

25. The present Convention, duly ratified, shall replace as between Contracting Powers, the Convention of the 29th July, 1899, for the adaptation to maritime warfare of the principles of the Geneva Convention.

The Convention of 1899 remains in force as between the Powers which signed it but which do not also ratify the present Convention.

26. The present Convention shall come into force, in the case of the Powers which were a party to the first deposit of ratifications, sixty days after the date of the *procès-verbal* of this deposit, and, in the case of the Powers which ratify subsequently or which adhere, sixty days after the notification of their ratification or of their adhesion has been received by the Netherland Government.

27. In the event of one of the Contracting Powers wishing to denounce the present Convention, the denunciation shall be notified in writing to the Netherland Government, which shall at once communicate a duly certified copy of the notification to all the other Powers, informing them at the same time of the date on which it was received.

The denunciation shall only have effect in regard to the notifying Power, and one year after the notification has reached the Netherland Government.

28. A register kept by the Netherland Ministry for Foreign Affairs shall give the date of the deposit of ratifications made in virtue of Article 23, paragraphs 3 and 4, as well as the date on which the notifications of adhesion (Article 24, paragraph 2) or of denunciation (Article 27, paragraph 1) have been received.

Each Contracting Power is entitled to have access to this register and to be supplied with duly certified extracts from it.

XVI. CONVENTION

RELATIVE TO CERTAIN RESTRICTIONS ON THE EXERCISE OF THE RIGHT OF CAPTURE IN MARITIME WAR.

2d PEACE CONFERENCE, THE HAGUE, 18 OCT. 1907, XI.

CHAPTER I.

POSTAL CORRESPONDENCE.

ART. 1. The postal correspondence of neutrals or belligerents, whatever its official or private character may be, found on the high seas on board a neutral or enemy ship, is inviolable. If the ship is detained, the correspondence is forwarded by the captor with the least possible delay.

The provisions of the preceding paragraph do not apply, in case of violation of blockade, to correspondence destined for or proceding from a blockaded port.

2. The inviolability of postal correspondence does not exempt a neutral mail-ship from the laws and customs of maritime war as to neutral merchant-ships in general. The ship, however, may not be searched except when absolutely necessary, and then only with as much consideration and expedition as possible.

CHAPTER II.

THE EXEMPTION FROM CAPTURE OF CERTAIN VESSELS.

3. Vessels used exclusively for fishing along the coast or small boats employed in local trade are exempt from capture, as well as their appliances, rigging, tackle, and cargo.

They cease to be exempt as soon as they take any part whatever in hostilities.

The Contracting Powers agree not to take advantage of the harmless character of the said vessels in order to use them for military purposes while preserving their peaceful appearance.

4. Vessels charged with religious, scientific, or philanthropic missions are likewise exempt from capture.

CHAPTER III.

REGULATIONS REGARDING THE CREWS OF ENEMY MERCHANT-SHIPS CAPTURED BY A BELLIGERENT.

5. When an enemy merchant-ship is captured by a belligerent, such of its crew as are nationals of a neutral State are not made prisoners of war.

The same rule applies in the case of the captain and officers, likewise nationals of a neutral State, if they promise formally in writing not to serve on an enemy ship while the war lasts.

6. The captain, officers, and members of the crew, when nationals of the enemy State, are not made prisoners of war, on condition that they make a formal promise in writing, not to undertake, while hostilities last, any service connected with the operations of the war.

7. The names of the persons retaining their liberty under the conditions laid down in Article 5, paragraph 2, and in Article 6, are notified by the belligerent captor to the other belligerent. The latter is forbidden knowingly to employ the said persons.

8. The provisions of the three preceding Articles do not apply to ships taking part in the hostilities.

CHAPTER IV.

Final Provisions.

9. The provisions of the present Convention do not apply except between Contracting Powers, and then only if all the belligerents are parties to the Convention.

Art. 10—14 = VII Art. 3—7

XVII. CONVENTION

RELATIVE TO THE ESTABLISHMENT OF AN INTERNATIONAL PRIZE COURT.

2d PEACE CONFERENCE, THE HAGUE, 18 OCT. 1907, XII.

PART I.

General Provisions.

Art. 1. The validity of the capture of a merchant-ship or its cargo is decided before a Prize Court in accordance with the present Convention when neutral or enemy property is involved.

2. Jurisdiction in matters of prize is exercised in the first instance by the Prize Courts of the belligerent captor.

The judgments of these Courts are pronounced in public or are officially notified to parties concerned who are neutrals or enemies.

3. The judgments of National Prize Courts may be brought before the International Prize Court:

1. When the judgment of the National Prize Courts affects the property of a neutral Power or individual;
2. When the judgment affects enemy property and relates to:
   a. Cargo on board a neutral ship;
   b. An enemy ship captured in the territorial waters of a neutral Power, when that Power has not made the capture the subject of a diplomatic claim;
   c. A claim based upon the allegation that the seizure has been effected in violation, either of the provisions of a Convention in force between the belligerent Powers, or of an enactment issued by the belligerent captor.

The appeal against the judgment of the National Court can be based on the ground that the judgment was wrong either in fact or in law.

4. An appeal may be brought:

1. By a neutral Power, if the judgment of the National Tribunals injuriously affects its property or the property of its nationals (Article 3, 1., or if the capture of an enemy vessel is alleged to have taken place in the territorial waters of that Power (Article 3, 2, b.);
2. By a neutral individual, if the judgment of the National Court injuriously affects his property (Article 3, 1), subject, however, to the reservation that the Power to which he belongs may forbid him to bring the case before the Court, or may itself undertake the proceedings in his place;
3. By an individual subject or citizen of an enemy Power, if the judg-

ment of the National Court injuriously affects his property in the cases referred to in Article 3, 2, except that mentioned in paragraph *b*.

5. An appeal may also be brought on the same conditions as in the preceding Article, by persons belonging either to neutral States or to the enemy, deriving their rights from and entitled to represent an individual qualified to appeal, and who have taken part in the proceedings before the National Court. Persons so entitled may appeal separately to the extent of their interest.

The same rule applies in the case of persons belonging either to neutral States or to the enemy who derive their rights from and are entitled to represent a neutral Power whose property was the subject of the decision.

6. When, in accordance with the above Article 3, the International Court has jurisdiction, the National Courts cannot deal with a case in more than two instances. The municipal law of the belligerent captor shall decide whether the case may be brought before the International Court after judgment has been given in first instance or only after an appeal.

If the National Courts fail to give final judgment within two years from the date of capture, the case may be carried direct to the International Court.

7. If a question of law to be decided is covered by a Treaty in force between the belligerent captor and a Power which is itself or whose subject or citizen is a party to the proceedings, the Court is governed by the provisions of the said Treaty.

In the absence of such provisions, the Court shall apply the rules of international law. If no generally recognized rule exists, the Court shall give judgment in accordance with the general principlés of justice and equity.

The above provisions apply equally to questions relating to the order and mode of proof.

If, in accordance with Article 3, 2, *c.*, the ground of appeal is the violation of an enactment issued by the belligerent captor, the Court will enforce the enactment.

The Court may disregard failure to comply with the procedure laid down in the enactments of the belligerent captor, when it is of opinion that the consequences of complying therewith are unjust and inequitable.

8. If the Court pronounces the capture of the vessel or cargo to be valid, they shall be disposed, of in accordance with the laws of the belligerent captor.

If it pronounces the capture to be null, the Court shall order restitution of the vessel or cargo, and shall fix, if there is occasion, the amount of the damages. If the vessel or cargo have been sold or destroyed, the Court shall determine the compensation to be given to the owner on this account.

If the national Court pronounced the capture to be null, the Court can only be asked to decide as to the damages.

9. The Contracting Powers undertake to submit in good faith to the decisions of the International Prize Court and to carry them out with the least possible delay.

PART II.

CONSTITUTION OF THE INTERNATIONAL PRIZE COURT.

10. The International Prize Court is composed of Judges and Deputy Judges, who will be appointed by the Contracting Powers, and must all be jurists of known proficiency in questions of international maritime law, and of the highest moral reputation.

The appointment of these Judges and Deputy Judges shall be made within six months after the ratification of the present Convention.

11. The Judges and Deputy Judges are appointed for a period of six years, reckoned from the date on which the notification of their appointment is received by the Administrative Council established by the Convention for the Pacific Settlement of International Disputes of the 29th July, 1899. Their appointments can be renewed.

Should one of the Judges or Deputy Judges die or resign, the same procedure is followed for filling the vacancy as was followed for appointing him. In this case, the appointment is made for a fresh period of six years.

12. The Judges of the International Prize Court are all equal in rank and have precedence according to the date on which the notification of their appointment was received(Article 11, paragraph 1), and if they sit by rota (Article 15, paragraph 2), according to the date on which they entered upon their duties. When the date is the same the senior in age takes precedence.

The Deputy Judges when acting are assimilated to the Judges. They rank, however, after them.

13. The Judges enjoy diplomatic privileges and immunities in the performance of their duties and when outside their own country.

Before taking their seat, the Judges must swear, or make a solemn promise before the Administrative Council, to discharge their duties impartially and conscientiously.

14. The Court is composed of fifteen Judges; nine Judges constitute a quorum.

A Judge who is absent or prevented from sitting is replaced by the Deputy Judge.

15. The Judges appointed by the following Contracting Powers: Germany, the United States of America, Austria-Hungary, France, Great Britain, Italy, Japan, and Russia, are always summoned to sit.

The Judges and Deputy Judges appointed by the other Contracting Powers sit by rota as shown in the Table annexed to the present Convention; their duties may be performed successively by the same person. The same Judge may be appointed by several of the said Powers.

16. If a belligerent Power has, according to the rota, no Judge sitting in the Court, it may ask that the Judge appointed by it should take part in the settlement of all cases arising from the war. Lots shall then be drawn as to which of the Judges entitled to sit according to the rota shall withdraw. This arrangement does not affect the Judge appointed by the other belligerent.

17. No Judge can sit who has been a party, in any way whatever, to the sentence pronounced by the National Courts, or has taken part in the case as counsel or advocate for one of the parties.

No Judge or Deputy Judge can, during his tenure of office, appear as agent or advocate before the International Prize Court, nor act for one of the parties in any capacity whatever.

18. The belligerent captor is entitled to appoint a naval officer of high rank to sit as Assessor, but with no voice in the decision. A neutral Power, which is a party to the proceedings or whose subject or citizen is a party, has the same right of appointment; if as the result of this last provision more than one Power is concerned, they must agree among themselves, if necessary by lot, on the officer to be appointed.

19. The Court elects its President and Vice-President by an absolute majority of the votes cast. After two ballots, the election is made by a bare majority, and, in case the votes are equal, by lot.

20. The Judges on the International Prize Court are entitled to travelling allowances in accordance with the regulations in force in their own country, and in addition receive, while the Court is sitting or while they are carrying out duties conferred upon them by the Court, a sum of 100 Netherland florins per diem.

These payments are included in the general expenses of the Court dealt with in Article 47, and are paid through the International Bureau established by the Convention of the 29th July, 1899.

The Judges may not receive from their own Government or from that of any other Power any remuneration in their capacity of members of the Court.

21. The seat of the International Prize Court is at The Hague and it cannot, except in the case of *force majeure*, be transferred elsewhere without the consent of the belligerents.

22. The Administrative Council fulfils, with regard to the International Prize Court, the same functions as to the Permanent Court of Arbitration, but only Representatives of Contracting Powers will be members of it.

23. The International Bureau acts as registry to the International Prize Court and must place its offices and staff at the disposal of the Court. It has charge of the archives and carries out the administrative work.

The Secretary-General of the International Bureau acts as Registrar.

The necessary secretaries to assist the Registrar, translators and shorthand writers are appointed and sworn in by the Court.

24. The Court determines which language it will itself use and what languages may be used before it, but the official language of the National Courts which have had cognizance of the case may always be used before the Court.

25. Powers which are concerned in a case may appoint special agents to act as intermediaries between themselves and the Court. They may also engage counsel or advocates to defend their rights and interests.

26. A private person concerned in a case will be represented before the

Court by an attorney, who must be either an advocate qualified to plead before a Court of Appeal or a High Court of one of the Contracting States, or a lawyer practising before a similar Court, or lastly, a professor of law at one of the higher teaching centres of those countries.

27. For all notices to be served, in particular on the parties, witnesses, or experts, the Court may apply direct to the Government of the State on whose territory the service is to be carried out. The same rule applies in the case of steps being taken to procure evidence.

The requests for this purpose are to be executed so far as the means at the disposal of the Power applied to under its municipal law allow. They cannot be rejected unless the Power in question considers them calculated to impair its sovereign rights or its safety. If the request is complied with, the fees charged must only comprise the expenses actually incurred.

The Court is equally entitled to act through the Power on whose territory it sits.

Notices to be given to parties in the place where the Court sits may be served through the International Bureau.

PART III.

Procedure in the International Prize Court.

28. An appeal to the International Prize Court is entered by means of a written declaration made in the National Court which has already dealt with the case or addressed to the International Bureau; in the latter case the appeal can be entered by telegram.

The period within which the appeal must be entered is fixed at 120 days, counting from the day the decision is delivered or notified (Article 2, paragraph 2).

29. If the notice of appeal is entered in the National Court, this Court, without considering the question whether the appeal was entered in due time, will transmit within seven days the record of the case to the International Bureau.

If the notice of appeal is sent to the International Bureau, the Bureau will immediately inform the National Court, when possible by telegraph. The latter will transmit the record as provided in the preceding paragraph.

When the appeal is brought by a neutral individual the International Bureau at once informs by telegraph the individual's Government, in order to enable it to enforce the rights it enjoys under Article 4, paragraph 2.

30. In the case provided for in Article 6, paragraph 2, the notice of appeal can be addressed to the International Bureau only. It must be entered within thirty days of the expiration of the period of two years.

31. If the appellant does not enter his appeal within the period laid down in Articles 28 or 30, it shall be rejected without discussion.

Provided that he can show that he was prevented from so doing by *force majeure*, and that the appeal was entered within sixty days after the circumstances which prevented him entering it before had ceased to operate, the Court can, after hearing the respondent, grant relief from the effect of the above provision.

32. If the appeal is entered in time, a certified copy of the notice of appeal is forthwith officially transmitted by the Court to the respondent.

33. If, in addition to the parties who are before the Court, there are other parties concerned who are entitled to appeal, or if, in the case referred to in Article 29, paragraph 3, the Government who has received notice of an appeal has not announced its decision, the Court will await before dealing with the case the expiration of the period laid down in Articles 28 or 30.

34. The procedure before the International Court includes two distinct parts: the written pleadings and oral discussions.

The written pleadings consist of the deposit and exchange of cases, counter-cases, and, if necessary, of replies, of which the order is fixed by the Court, as also the periods within which they must be delivered. The parties annex thereto all papers and documents of which they intend to make use.

A certified copy of every document produced by one party must be communicated to the other party through the medium of the Court.

35. After the close of the pleadings, a public sitting is held on a day fixed by the Court.

At this sitting the parties state their view of the case both as to the law and as to the facts.

The Court may, at any stage of the proceedings, suspend speeches of counsel, either at the request of one of the parties, or on their own initiative, in order that supplementary evidence may be obtained.

36. The International Court may order the supplementary evidence to be taken either in the manner provided by Article 27, or before itself, or one or more of the members of the Court, provided that this can be done without resort to compulsion or the use of threats.

If steps are to be taken for the purpose of obtaining evidence by members of the Court outside the territory where it is sitting, the consent of the foreign Government must be obtained.

37. The parties are summoned to take part in all stages of the proceedings and receive certified copies of the Minutes.

38. The discussions are under the control of the President or Vice-President, or, in case they are absent or cannot act, of the senior Judge present.

The Judge appointed by a belligerent party cannot preside.

39. The discussions take place in public, subject to the right of a Government who is a party to the case to demand that they be held in private.

Minutes are taken of these discussions and signed by the President and Registrar, and these Minutes alone have an authentic character.

40. If a party does not appear, despite the fact that he has been duly cited, or if a party fails to comply with some step within the period fixed by the Court, the case proceeds without that party, and the Court gives judgment in accordance with the material at its disposal.

41. The Court officially notifies to the parties Decrees or decisions made in their absence.

42. The Court takes into consideration in arriving at its decision all the facts, evidence, and oral statements.

43. The Court considers its decision in private and the proceedings are secret.

All questions are decided by a majority of the Judges present. If the number of Judges is even and equally divided, the vote of the junior Judge in the order of precedence laid down in Article 12, paragraph 1, is not counted.

44. The judgment of the Court must give the reasons on which it is based. It contains the names of the Judges taking part in it, and also of the Assessors, if any; it is signed by the President and Registrar.

45. The sentence is pronounced in public sitting, the parties concerned being present or duly summoned to attend; the sentence is officially communicated to the parties.

When this communication has been made, the Court transmits to the National Prize Court the record of the case, together with copies of the various decisions arrived at and of the Minutes of the proceedings.

46. Each party pays its own costs.

The party against whom the Court decides bears, in addition, the costs of the trial, and also pays 1 per cent. of the value of the subject-matter of the case as a contribution to the general expenses of the International Court. The amount of these payments is fixed in the judgment of the Court.

If the appeal is brought by an individual, he will furnish the International Bureau with security to an amount fixed by the Court, for the purpose of guaranteeing eventual fulfilment of the two obligations mentioned in the preceding paragraph. The Court is entitled to postpone the opening of the proceedings until the security has been furnished.

47. The general expenses of the International Prize Court are borne by the Contracting Powers in proportion to their share in the composition of the Court as laid down in Article 15 and in the annexed Table. The appointment of Deputy Judges does not involve any contribution.

The Administrative Council applies to the Powers for the funds requisite for the working of the Court.

48. When the Court is not sitting, the duties conferred upon it by Article 32, Article 34, paragraphs 2 and 3, Article 35, paragraph 1, and Article 46, paragraph 3, are discharged by a delegation of three Judges appointed by the Court. This delegation decides by a majority of votes.

49. The Court itself draws up its own rules of procedure, which must be communicated to the Contracting Powers.

It will meet to elaborate these rules within a year of the ratification of the present Convention.

50. The Court may propose modifications in the provisions of the present Convention concerning procedure. These proposals are communicated, through the medium of the Netherland Government, to the Contracting Powers, which will consider together as to the measures to be taken.

PART IV.

Final Provisions.

51. The present Convention does not apply as of right except when the belligerent Powers are all parties to the Convention.

It is further fully understood that an appeal to the International Prize Court can only be brought by a Contracting Power or the subject or citizen of a Contracting Power.

In the cases mentioned in Article 5, the appeal is only admitted when both the owner and the person entitled to represent him are equally Contracting Powers or the subjects or citizens of Contracting Powers.

52. The present Convention shall be ratified and the ratifications shall be deposited at The Hague as soon as all the Powers mentioned in Article 15 and in the Table annexed are in a position to do so.

The deposit of the ratifications shall take place, in any case, on the 30th June, 1909, if the Powers which are ready to ratify furnish nine Judges and nine Deputy Judges to the Court, qualified to validly constitute a Court. If not, the deposit shall be postponed until this condition is fulfilled.

A Minute of the deposit of ratifications shall be drawn up, of which a certified copy shall be forwarded, through the diplomatic channel, to each of the Powers referred to in the first paragraph.

53. The Powers referred to in Article 15 and in the Table annexed are entitled to sign the present Convention up to the deposit of the ratifications contemplated in paragraph 2 of the preceding Article.

After this deposit, they can at any time adhere to it, purely and simply. A Power wishing to adhere, notifies its intention in writing to the Netherland Government transmitting to it, at the same time, the act of adhesion, which shall be deposited in the archives of the said Government. The latter shall send, through the diplomatic channel, a certified copy of the notification and of the act of adhesion to all the Powers referred to in the preceding paragraph, informing them of the date on which it has received the notification.

45. The present Convention shall come into force six months from the deposit of the ratifications contemplated in Article 52, paragraphs 1 and 2.

The adhesions shall take effect sixty days after notification of such adhesion has been received by the Netherland Government, or as soon as possible on the expiration of the period contemplated in the preceding paragraph.

The International Court shall, however, have jurisdiction to deal with prize cases decided by the National Courts at any time after the deposit of the ratifications or of the receipt of the notification of the adhesions. In such cases, the period fixed in Article 28, paragraph 2, shall only be reckoned from the date when the Convention comes into force as regards a Power which has ratified or adhered.

55. The present Convention shall remain in force for twelve years from the time it comes into force, as determined by Article 54, paragraph 1, even in the case of Powers which adhere subsequently.

It shall be renewed tacitly from six years to six years unless denounced.

Denunciation must be notified in writing, at least one year before the expiration of each of the periods mentioned in the two preceding paragraphs, to the Netherland Government, which will inform all the other Contracting Powers.

Denunciation shall only take effect in regard to the Power which has notified it. The Convention shall remain in force in the case of the other Contracting Powers, provided that their participation in the appointment of Judges is sufficient to allow of the composition of the Court with nine Judges and nine Deputy Judges.

56. In case the present Convention is not in operation as regards all the Powers referred to in Article 15 and the annexed Table, the Administrative Council shall drawn up a list on the lines of that Article and Table of the Judges and Deputy Judges through whom the Contracting Powers will share in the composition of the Court. The times allotted by the said Table to Judges who are summoned to sit in rota will be redistributed between the different years of the six-year period in such a way that, as far as possible, the number of the Judges of the Court in each year shall be the same. If the number of Deputy Judges is greater than that of the Judges, the number of the latter can be completed by Deputy Judges chosen by lot among those Powers which do not nominate a Judge.

The list drawn up in this way by the Administrative Council shall be notified to the Contracting Powers. It shall be revised when the number of these Powers is modified as the result of adhesions or denunciations.

The change resulting from an adhesion is not made until the 1st January after the date on which the adhesion takes effect, unless the adhering Power is a belligerent Power, in which case it can ask to be at once represented in the Court, the provision of Article 16 being, moreover, applicable if necessary.

When the total number of Judges is less than eleven, seven Judges form a quorum.

57. Two years before the expiration of each period referred to in paragraphs 1 and 2 of Article 55 any Contracting Power can demand a modification of the provisions of Article 15 and of the annexed Table, relative to its participation in the composition of the Court. The demand shall be addressed to the Administrative Council, which will examine it and submit to all the Powers proposals as to the measures to be adopted. The Powers shall inform the Administrative Council of their decision with the least possible delay. The result shall be at once, and at least one year and thirty days before the expiration of the said period of two years, communicated to the Power which made the demand.

When necessary, the modifications adopted by the Powers shall come into force from the commencement of the fresh period.

In faith whereof the Plenipotentiaries have appended their signatures to the present Convention.

Done at The Hague, the 18th October, 1907, in a single copy, which shall remain deposited in the archives of the Netherland Government, and duly certified copies of which shall be sent, through the diplomatic channel, to the Powers designated in Article 15 and in the Table annexed.

Annex to Article 15.

DISTRIBUTION OF JUDGES AND DEPUTY JUDGES BY COUNTRIES FOR EACH YEAR OF THE PERIOD OF SIX YEARS.

	Judges.	Deputy Judges.		Judges.	Deputy Judges.
	First Year.			Second Year.	
1	Argentina	Paraguay	1	Argentina	Panama
2	Colombia	Bolivia	2	Spain	Spain
3	Spain	Spain	3	Greece	Roumania
4	Greece	Roumania	4	Norway	Sweden.
5	Norway	Sweden	5	Netherlands	Belgium
6	Netherlands	Belgium	6	Turkey	Luxemburg
7	Turkey	Persia	7	Uruguay	Costa Rica
	Third Year.			Fourth Year.	
1	Brazil	Santo Domingo.	1	Brazil	Guatemala
2	China	Turkey	2	China	Turkey
3	Spain	Portugal.	3	Spain	Portugal
4	Netherlands	Switzerland	4	Peru	Honduras
5	Roumania	Greece	5	Roumania	Greece
6	Sweden	Denmark	6	Sweden	Denmark
7	Venezuela	Haïti.	7	Switzerland	Netherlands
	Fifth Year.			Sixth Year.	
1	Belgium	Netherlands	1	Belgium	Netherlands
2	Bulgaria	Montenegro	2	Chile	Salvador
3	Chile	Nicaragua	3	Denmark	Norway
4	Denmark	Norway	4	Mexico	Ecuador
5	Mexico	Cuba	5	Portugal	Spain
6	Persia	China	6	Servia	Bulgaria
7	Portugal	Spain	7	Siam	China

XVIII. CONVENTION

RESPECTING THE RIGHTS AND DUTIES OF NEUTRAL POWERS IN NAVAL WAR.

2d PEACE CONFERENCE, THE HAGUE, 18 OCT. 1907. XIII.

ART. 1. Belligerents are bound to respect the sovereign rights of neutral Powers and to abstain, in neutral territory or neutral waters, from any act which would, if knowingly permitted by any Power, constitute a violation of neutrality.

2. Any act of hostility, including capture and the exercise of the right of search, committed by belligerent war-ships in the territorial waters of a neutral Power, constitutes a violation of neutrality and is strictly forbidden.

3. When a ship has been captured in the territorial waters of a neutral Power, this Power must employ, if the prize is still within its jurisdiction, the means at its disposal to release the prize with its officers and crew, and to intern the prize crew.

If the prize is not in the jurisdiction of the neutral Power, the captor Government, on the demand of that Power, must liberate the prize with its officers and crew.

4. A Prize Court cannot be set up by a belligerent on neutral territory or on a vessel in neutral waters.

5. Belligerents are forbidden to use neutral ports and waters as a base of naval operations against their adversaries, and in particular to erect wireless telegraphy stations or any apparatus for the purpose of communicating with the belligerent forces on land or sea.

6. The supply, in any manner, directly or indirectly, by a neutral Power to a belligerent Power, of war-ships, ammunition, or war material of any kind whatever, is forbidden.

7. A neutral Power is not bound to prevent the export or transit, for the use of either belligerent, of arms, ammunitions, or, in general, of anything which could be of use to an army or fleet.

8. A neutral Government is bound to employ the means at its disposal to prevent the fitting out or arming of any vessel within its jurisdiction which it has reason to believe is intended to cruise, or engage in hostile operations, against a Power with which that Government is at peace. It is also bound to display the same vigilance to prevent the departure from its jurisdiction of any vessel intended to cruise, or engage in hostile operations, which had been adapted entirely or partly within the said jurisdiction for use in war.

9. A neutral Power must apply impartially to the two belligerents the conditions, restrictions, or prohibitions made by it in regard to the ad-

mission into its ports, roadsteads, or territorial waters, of belligerent war-ships or of their prizes.

Nevertheless, a neutral Power may forbid a belligerent vessel which has failed to conform to the orders and regulations made by it, or which has violated neutrality, to enter its ports or roadsteads.

10. The neutrality of a Power is not affected by the mere passage through its territorial waters of war-ships or prizes belonging to belligerents.

11. A neutral Power may allow belligerent war-ships to employ its licensed pilots.

12. In the absence of special provisions to the contrary in the legislation of a neutral Power, belligerent war-ships are not permitted to remain in the ports, roadsteads, or territorial waters of the said Power for more than twenty-four hours, except in the cases covered by the present Convention.

13. If a Power which has been informed of the outbreak of hostilities learns that a belligerent war-ship is in one of its ports or roadsteads, or in its territorial waters, it must notify the said ship to depart within twenty-four hours or within the time prescribed by local regulations.

14. A belligerent war-ship may not prolong its stay in a neutral port beyond the permissible time except on account of damage or stress of weather. It must depart as soon as the cause of the delay is at an end.

The regulations as to the question of the length of time which these vessels may remain in neutral ports, roadsteads, or waters, do not apply to war-ships devoted exclusively to religious, scientific, or philantropic purposes.

15. In the absence of special provisions to the contrary in the legislation of a neutral Power, the maximum number of war-ships belonging to a belligerent which may be in one of the ports or roadsteads of that Power simultaneously shall be three.

16. When war-ships belonging to both belligerents are present simultaneously in a neutral port or roadstead, a period of not less than twenty-four hours must elapse between the departure of the ship belonging to one belligerent and the departure of the ship belonging to the other.

The order of departure is determined by the order of arrival, unless the ship which arrived first is so circumstanced that an extension of its stay is permissible.

A belligerent war-ship may not leave a neutral port or roadstead until twenty-four hours after the departure of a merchant-ship flying the flag of its adversary.

17. In neutral ports and roadsteads belligerent war-ships may only carry out such repairs as are absolutely necessary to render them seaworthy, and may not add in any manner whatsoever to their fighting force. The local authorities of the neutral Power shall decide what repairs are necessary, and these must be carried out with the least possible delay.

18. Belligerent war-ships may not make use of neutral ports, roadsteads, on territorial waters for replenishing or increasing their supplies of war material or their armament, or for completing their crews.

19. Belligerent war-ships may only revictual in neutral ports or roadsteads to bring up their supplies to the peace standard.

Similarly these vessels may only ship sufficient fuel to enable them to reach the nearest port in their own country. They may, on the other hand, fill up their bunkers built to carry fuel, when in neutral countries which have adopted this method of determining the amount of fuel to be supplied.

If, in accordance with the law of the neutral Power the ships are not supplied with coal within twenty-four hours of their arrival, the permissible duration of their stay is extended by twenty-four hours.

20. Belligerent war-ships which have shipped fuel in a port belonging to a neutral Power may not within the succeeding three months replenish their supply in a port of the same Power.

21. A prize may only be brought into a neutral port on account of unseaworthiness, stress of weather, or want of fuel or provisions.

It must leave as soon as the circumstances which justified its entry are at an end. If it does not, the neutral Power must order it to leave at once; should it fail to obey, the neutral Power must employ the means at its disposal to release it with its officers and crew and to intern the prize crew.

22. A neutral Power must, similarly, release a prize brought into one of its ports under circumstances other than those referred to in Article 21.

23. A neutral Power may allow prizes to enter its ports and roadsteads, whether under convoy or not, when they are brought there to be sequestrated pending the decision of a Prize Court. It may have the prize taken to another of its ports.

If the prize is couvoyed by a war-ship, the prize crew may go on board the convoying ship.

If the prize is not under convoy, the prize crew are left at liberty.

24. If, notwithstanding the notification of the neutral Power, a belligerent ship of war does not leave a port where it is not entitled to remain, the neutral Power is entitled to take such measures as it considers necessary to render the ship incapable of taking the sea during the war, and the commanding officer of the ship must facilitate the execution of such measures.

When a belligerent ship is detained by a neutral Power, the officers and crew are likewise detained.

The officers and crew thus detained may be left in the ship or kept either on another vessel or on land, and may be subjected to the measures of restriction which it may appear necessary to impose upon them. A sufficient number of men for looking after the vessel must, however, be always left on board.

The officers may be left at liberty on giving their word not to quit the neutral territory without permission.

25. A neutral Power is bound to exercise such surveillance as the means at its disposal allow to prevent any violation of the provisions of the above Articles occurring in its ports or roadsteads or in its waters.

26. The exercise by a neutral Power of the rights laid down in the present Convention can under no circumstances be considered as an unfriendly act by one or other belligerent who has accepted the Article relating thereto.

27. The Contracting Powers shall communicate to each other in due course all Laws, Proclamations, and other enactments regulating in their respective countries the status of belligerent war-ships in their ports and waters, by means of a communication addressed to the Government of the Netherlands, and forwarded immediately by that Government to the other Contracting Powers.

28. The provisions of the present Convention do not apply except to the Contracting Powers, and then only if all the belligerents are parties to the Convention.

Art, 29—33 = VII Art. 3—7.

XIX. DECLARATION

PROHIBITING THE DISCHARGE OF PROJECTILES AND EXPLOSIVES FROM BALLONS.

The Undersigned, Plenipotentiaries of the Powers invited to the Second International Peace Conference at The Hague, duly authorized to that effect by their Governments, inspired by the sentiments which found expression in the Declaration of St. Petersburg of the 29th November (11th December), 1868, and being desirous of renewing the declaration of The Hague of the 29th July, 1899, which has now expired,

Declare:

The Contracting Powers agree to prohibit, for a period extending to the close of the Third Peace Conference, the discharge of projectiles and explosives from balloons or by other new methods of a similar nature.

The present Declaration is only binding on the Contracting Powers in case of war between two or more of them.

It shall cease to be binding from the time when, in a war between the Contracting Powers, one of the belligerents is joined by a non-Contracting Power.

The present Declaration shall be ratified as soon as possible.

The ratifications shall be deposited at The Hague.

A *procès-verbal* shall be drawn up recording the receipt of the ratifications, of which a duly certified copy shall be sent, through the diplomatic channel, to all the Contracting Powers.

Non-Signatory Powers may adhere to the present Declaration. To do so, they must make known their adhesion to the Contracting Powers by means of a written notification, addressed to the Netherland Government, and communicated by it to all the other Contracting Powers.

In the event of one of the High Contracting Parties denouncing the present Declaration, such denunciation shall not take effect until a year after the notification made in writing to the Netherland Government, and forthwith communicated by it to all the other Contracting Powers.

This denunciation shall only have affect in regard to the notifying Power.

XX. DECLARATION OF LONDON
CONCERNING THE LAW OF NAVAL WAR.

FEBR. 26. 1909.

CHAPTER I.

BLOCKADE IN TIME OF WAR.

ART. 1. A blockade must not extend beyond the ports and coasts belonging to or occupied by the enemy.

2. In accordance with the Declaration of Paris of 1856, a blockade, in order to be binding, must be effective— that is to say, it must be maintained by a force sufficient really to prevent access to the enemy coast-line.

3. The question whether a blockade is effective is a question of fact.

4. A blockade is not regarded as raised if the blockading force is temporarily withdrawn on account of stress of weather.

5. A blockade must be applied impartially to the ships of all nations.

6. The commander of a blockading force may give permission to a warship to enter, and subsequently to leave, a blockaded port.

7. In circumstances of distress, acknowledged by an officer of the blockading force, a neutral vessel may enter a place under blockade and subsequently leave it, provided that she has neither discharged nor shipped any cargo there.

8. A blockade, in order to be binding, must be declared in accordance with Art. 9, and notified in accordance with Arts. 11 and 16.

9. A declaration of blockade is made either by the blockading Power or by the naval authorities acting in its name.

It specifies:

1. The date when the blockade begins;
2. The geographical limits of the coast-line under blockade;
3. The period within which neutral vessels may come out.

10. If the operations of the blockading Power, or of the naval authorities acting in its name, do not tally with the particulars, which, in accordance with Art. 9, 1 and 2, must be inserted in the declaration of blockade, the declaration is void, and a new declaration is necessary in order to make the blockade operative.

11. A declaration of blockade is notified:

1. To neutral Powers, by the blockading Power by means of a communication addressed to the Governments direct, or to their representatives accredited to it;
2. To the local authorities, by the officer commanding the blockading force. The local authorities will in turn inform the foreign consular

officers at the port or on the coast-line under blockade as soon as possible.

12. The rules as to declaration and notification of blockade apply to cases where the limits of a blockade are extended, or where a blockade is re-established after having been raised.

13. The voluntary raising of a blockade, as also any restriction in the limits of a blockade, must be notified in the manner prescribed by Art. 11.

14. The liability of a neutral vessel to capture for breach of blockade is contingent on her knowledge, actual or presumptive, of the blockade.

15. Failing proof to the contrary, knowledge of the blockade is presumed if the vessel left a neutral port subsequently to the notification of the blockade to the Power to which such port belongs, provided that such notification was made in sufficient time.

16. If a vessel approaching a blockaded port has no knowledge, actual or presumptive, of the blockade, the notification must be made to the vessel itself by an officer of one of the ships of the blockading force. This notification should be entered in the vessel's log-book, and must state the day and hour, and the geographical position of the vessel at the time.

If through the negligence of the officer commanding the blockading force no declaration of blockade has been notified to the local authorities, or, if in the declaration, as notified, no period has been mentioned within which neutral vessels may come out, a neutral vessel coming out of the blockaded port must be allowed to pass free.

17. Neutral vessels may not be captured for breach of blockade except within the area of operations of the warships detailed to render the blockade effective.

18. The blockading forces must not bar access to neutral ports or coasts.

19. Whatever may be the ulterior destination of a vessel or of her cargo, she cannot be captured for breach of blockade, if at the moment, she is on her way to a non-blockaded port.

20. A vessel which has broken blockade outwards, or which has attempted to break blockade inwards, is liable to capture so long as she is pursued by a ship of the blockading force. If the pursuit is abandoned, or if the blockade is raised, her capture can no longer be effected.

21. A vessel found guilty of breach of blockade is liable to condemnation. The cargo is also condemned, unless it is proved that at the time of the shipment of the goods the shipper neither knew nor could have known of the intention to break the blockade.

CHAPTER II.

CONTRABAND OF WAR.

22. The following articles may, without notice, be treated as contraband of war, under the name of absolute contraband:

1. Arms of all kinds, including arms for sporting purposes, and their distinctive component parts.

2. Projectiles, charges, and cartridges of all kinds, and their distinctive component parts.
3. Powder and explosives specially prepared for use in war.
4. Gun-mountings, limber boxes, limbers, military waggons, field forges, and their distinctive component parts.
5. Clothing and equipment of a distinctively military character.
6. All kinds of harness of a distinctively military character.
7. Saddle, draught, and pack animals suitable for use in war.
8. Articles of camp equipment, and their distinctive component parts.
9. Armour plates.
10. Warships, including boats, and their distinctive component parts of such a nature that they can only be used on a vessel of war.
11. Implements and apparatus designed exclusively for the manufacture of munitions of war, for the manufacture or repair of arms, or war material for use on land or sea.

23. Articles exclusively used for war may be added to the list of absolute contraband by a declaration, which must be notified.

Such notification must be addressed to the Governments of other Powers, or to their representatives accredited to the Power making the declaration. A notification made after the outbreak of hostilities is addressed only to neutral Powers.

24. The following articles, susceptible of use in war as well as for purposes of peace, may, without notice, be treated as contraband of war, under the name of conditional contraband:

1. Foodstuffs.
2. Forage and grain, suitable for feeding animals.
3. Clothing, fabrics for clothing, and boots and shoes, suitable for use in war.
4. Gold and silver in coin or bullion; paper money.
5. Vehicles of all kinds available for use in war, and their component parts.
6. Vessels, craft, and boats of all kinds; floating docks, parts of docks and their component parts.
7. Railway material, both fixed and rolling-stock, and material for telegraphs, wireless telegraphs, and telephones.
8. Balloons and flying machines and their distinctive component parts, together with accessories and articles recognizable as intended for use in connection with balloons and flying machines.
9. Fuel; lubricants.
10. Powder and explosives not specially prepared for use in war.
11. Barbed wire and implements for fixing and cutting the same.
12. Horseshoes and shoeing materials.
13. Harness and saddlery.
14. Field-glasses, telescopes, chronometers, and all kinds of nautical instruments.

25. Articles susceptible of use in war as well as for purposes of peace, other than those enumerated in Arts. 22 and 24, may be added to the list of conditional contraband by a declaration, which must be notified in the manner provided for in the second paragraph of Art. 23.

26. If a Power waives, so far as it is concerned, the right to treat as contraband of war an article comprised in any of the classes enumerated in Arts. 22 and 24, such intention shall be announced by a declaration, which must be notified in the manner provided for in the second paragraph of Art. 23.

27. Articles which are not susceptible of use in war may not be declared contraband of war.

28. The following may not be declared contraband of war:

1 Raw cotton, wool, silk, jute, flax, hemp, and other raw materials of the textile industries, and yarns of the same.
2. Oil seeds and nuts; copra.
3. Rubber, resins, gums, and lacs; hops.
4. Raw hides and horns, bones, and ivory.
5. Natural and artificial manures, including nitrates and phosphates for agricultural purposes.
6. Metallic ores.
7. Earths, clays, lime, chalk, stone, including marble, bricks, slates, and tiles.
8. Chinaware and glass.
9. Paper and paper-making materials.
10. Soap, paint and colours, including articles exclusively used in their manufacture, and varnish.
11. Bleaching-powder, soda ash, caustic soda, salt cake, ammonia, sulphate of ammonia, and sulphate of copper.
12. Agricultural, mining, textile, and printing machinery.
13. Precious and semi-precious stones, pearls, mother-of-pearl, and coral.
14. Clocks and watches, other than chronometers.
15. Fashion and fancy goods.
16. Feathers of all kinds, hairs and bristles.
17. Articles of household furniture and decoration; office furniture and requisites.

29. Likewise the following may not be treated as contraband of war:

1. Articles serving exclusively to aid the sick and wounded. They can, however, in case of urgent military necessity and subject to the payment of compensation, be requisitioned, if their destination is that specified in Art. 30.
2. Articles intended for the use of the vessel in which they are found, as well as those intended for the use of her crew and passengers during the voyage.

30. Absolute contraband is liable to capture if it is shown to be destined to territory belonging to or occupied by the enemy, or to the armed forces of the enemy. It is immaterial whether the carriage of the goods is direct or entails transhipment or a subsequent transport by land.

31. Proof of the destination specified in Art. 30 is complete in the following cases:

1. When the goods are documented for discharge in an enemy port, or for delivery to the armed forces of the enemy.
2. When the vessel is to call at enemy ports only, or when she is to touch at an enemy port or meet the armed forces of the enemy before reaching the neutral port for which the goods in question are documented.

32. Where a vessel is carrying absolute contraband, her papers are conclusive proof as to the voyage on which she is engaged, unless she is found clearly out of the course indicated by her papers and unable to give adequate reasons to justify such deviation.

33. Conditional contraband is liable to capture if it is shown to be destined for the use of the armed forces or of a Government department of the enemy State, unless in this latter case the circumstances show that the goods cannot in fact be used for the purposes of the war in progress. This latter exception does not apply to a consignment coming under Art. 24, 4.

34. The destination referred to in Article 33 is presumed to exist if the goods are consigned to enemy authorities, or to a contractor established in the enemy country who, as a matter of common knowledge, supplies articles of this kind to the enemy. A similar presumption arises if the goods are consigned to a fortified place belonging to the enemy, or other place serving as a base for the armed forces of the enemy. No such presumption, however, arises in the case of a merchant vessel bound for one of these places if it is sought to prove that she herself is contraband.

In cases where the above presumptions do not arise the destination is presumed to be innocent.

The presumptions set up by this Article may be rebutted.

35. Conditional contraband is not liable to capture, except when found on board a vessel bound for territory belonging to or occupied by the enemy, or for the armed forces of the enemy, and when, it is not to be discharged in an intervening neutral port.

The ship's papers are conclusive proof both as to the voyage on which the vessel is engaged and as to the port of discharge of the goods, unless she is found clearly out of the course indicated by her papers, and unable to give adequate reasons to justify such deviation.

36. Notwithstanding the provisions of Art. 35, conditional contraband, if shown to have the destination referred to in Art. 33, is liable to capture in cases where the enemy country has no seaboard.

37. A vessel carrying goods liable to capture as absolute or conditional contraband may be captured on the high seas or in the territorial waters of the belligerents throughout the whole of her voyage, even if she is to touch at a port of call before reaching the hostile destination.

38. A vessel may not be captured on the ground that she has carried contraband on a previous occasion if such carriage is in point of fact at an end.

39. Contraband goods are liable to condemnation.

40. A vessel carrying contraband may be condemned if the contraband, reckoned either by value, weight, volume, or freight, forms more than half the cargo.

41. If a vessel carrying contraband is released, she may be condemned to pay the costs and expenses incurred by the captor in respect of the proceedings in the national prize court and the custody of the ship and cargo during the proceedings.

42. Goods which belong to the owner of the contraband and are on board the same vessel are liable to condemnation.

43. If a vessel is encountered at sea while unaware of the outbreak of hostilities or of the declaration of contraband which applies to her cargo, the contraband cannot be condemned except on payment of compensation; the vessel herself and the remainder of the cargo are not liable to condemnation or to the costs and expenses referred to in Art. 41. The same rule applies if the master after becoming aware of the outbreak of hostilities, or of the declaration of contraband, has had no opportunity of discharging the contraband.

A vessel is deemed to be aware of the existence of a state of war, or of a declaration of contraband, if she left a neutral port subsequently to the notification to the Power to which such port belongs of the outbreak of hostilities or of the declaration of contraband respectively, provided that such notification was made in sufficient time. A vessel is also deemed to be aware of the existence of a state of war if she left an enemy port after the outbreak of hostilities.

44. A vessel which has been stopped on the ground that she is carrying contraband, and which is not liable to condemnation on account of the proportion of contraband on board, may, when the circumstances permit, be allowed to continue her voyage if the master is willing to hand over the contraband to the belligerent warship.

The delivery of the contraband must be entered by the captor on the logbook of the vessel stopped, and the master must give the captor duly certified copies of all relevant papers.

The captor is at liberty to destroy the contraband that has been handed over to him under these conditions.

CHAPTER III.

Unneutral Service.

45. A neutral vessel will be condemned and will, in a general way, receive the same treatment as a neutral vessel liable to condemnation for carriage of contraband:

1. If she is on a voyage specially undertaken with a view to the transport of individual passengers who are embodied in the armed forces of the enemy, or with a view to the transmission of intelligence in the interests of the enemy.
2. If, to the knowledge of either the owner, the charterer, or the master, she is transporting a military detachment of the enemy, or one or

more persons who, in the course of the voyage, directly assist the operations of the enemy.

In the cases specified under the above heads, goods belonging to the owner of the vessel are likewise liable to condemnation.

The provisions of the present Article do not apply if the vessel is encountered at sea while unaware of the outbreak of hostilities, or if the master, after becoming aware of the outbreak of hostilities, has had no opportunity of disembarking the passengers. The vessel is deemed to be aware of the existence of a state of war if she left an enemy port subsequently to the outbreak of hostilities, or a neutral port subsequently to the notification of the outbreak of hostilities to the Power to which such port belongs, provided that such notification was made in sufficient time.

46. A neutral vessel will be condemned, and in a general way, receive the same treatment as would be applicable to her if she were an enemy merchant vessel:

1. If she takes a direct part in the hostilities;
2. If she is under the orders or control of an agent placed on board by the enemy Government;
3. If she is in the exclusive employment of the enemy Government;
4. If she is exclusively engaded at the time either in the transport of enemy troops or in the transmission of intelligence in the interest of the enemy.

In the cases covered by the present Article, goods belonging to the owner of the vessel are likewise liable to condemnation.

47. Any individual embodied in the armed forces of the enemy who is found on board a neutral merchant vessel, may be made a prisoner of war, even though there be no ground for the capture of the vessel.

CHAPTER IV.

Destruction of Neutral Prizes.

48. A neutral vessel which has been captured may not be destroyed by the captor; she must be taken into such port as is proper for the determination there of all questions concerning the validity of the capture.

49. As an exception, a neutral vessel which has been captured by a belligerent warship, and which would be liable to condemnation, may be destroyed if the observance of Art. 48 would involve danger to the safety of the warship or to the success of the operations in which she is engaged at the time.

50. Before the vessel is destroyed all persons on board must be placed in safety, and all the ship's papers and other documents which the parties interested consider relevant for the purpose of deciding on the validity of the capture must be taken on board the warship.

51. A captor who has destroyed a neutral vessel must, prior to any decision respecting the validity of the prize, establish that he only acted in the face of an exceptional necessity of the nature contemplated in Art. 49. If he fails to do this, he must compensate the parties interested and no examination shall be made of the question whether the capture was valid or not.

52. If the capture of a neutral vessel is subsequently held to be invalid, though the act of destruction has been held to have been justifiable, the captor must pay compensation to the parties interested, in place of the restitution to which they would have been entitled.

53. If neutral goods not liable to condemnation have been destroyed with the vessel, the owner of such goods is entitled to compensation.

54. The captor has the right to demand the handing over, or to proceed himself to the destruction of, any goods liable to condemnation found on board a vessel not herself liable to condemnation, provided that the circumstances are such as would, under Art. 49, justify the destruction of a vessel herself liable to condemnation. The captor must enter the goods surrendered or destroyed in the logbook of the vessel stopped, and must obtain duly certified copies of all relevant papers. When the goods have been handed over or destroyed, and the formalities duly carried out, the master must be allowed to continue his voyage.

The provisions of Arts. 51 and 52 respecting the obligations of a captor who has destroyed a neutral vessel are applicable.

CHAPTER V.

Transfer to a Neutral Flag.

55. The transfer of an enemy vessel to a neutral flag, effected before the outbreak of histilities is valid, unless it is proved that such transfer was made in order to evade the consequences to which an enemy vessel, as such, is exposed. There is, however, a presumption, if the bill of sale is not on board a vessel which has lost her belligerent nationality less than sixty days before the outbreak of hostilities, that the transfer is void. This presumption may be rebutted.

Where the transfer was effected more than thirty days before the outbreak of hostilities, there is an absolute presumption that it is valid if it is unconditional, complete, and in conformity with the laws of the countries concerned, and if its effect is such that neither the control of, nor the profits arising from the employment of, the vessel remain in the same hands as before the transfer. If, however, the vessel lost her belligerent nationality less than sixty days before the outbreak of hostilities and if the bill of sale is not on board, the capture of the vessel gives no right to damages.

56. The transfer of an enemy vessel to a neutral flag, effected after the outbreak of hostilities, is void unless it is proved that such transfer was not made in order to evade the consequences to which an enemy vessel, as such, is exposed.

There, however, is an absolute presumption that a transfer is void:

1. If the transfer has been made during a voyage or in a blockaded port.
2. If a right to repurchase or recover the vessel is reserved to the vendor,

3. If the requirements of the municipal law governing the right to fly the flag under which the vessel is sailing, have not been fulfilled.

CHAPTER VI.

Enemy Character.

57. Subject to the provisions respecting transfer to another flag, the neutral or enemy character of a vessel is determined by the flag which she is entitled to fly.

The case where a neutral vessel is engaged in a trade which is closed in time of peace, remains outside the scope of, and is in no wise affected by, this rule.

58. The neutral or enemy character of goods found on board an enemy vessel is determined by the neutral or enemy character of the owner.

59. In the absence of proof of the neutral character of goods found on board an enemy vessel, they are presumed to be enemy goods.

60. Enemy goods on board an enemy vessel retain their enemy character until they reach their destination, notwithstanding any transfer effected after the outbreak of hostilities while the goods are being forwarded.

If, however, prior to the capture, a former neutral owner exercises, on the bankruptcy of an existing enemy owner, a recognized legal right to recover the goods, they regain their neutral character.

CHAPTER VII.

Convoy.

61. Neutral vessels under national convoy are exempt from search. The commander of a convoy gives, in writing, at the request of the commander of a belligerent warship, all information as to the character of the vessels and their cargoes, which could be obtained by search.

62. If the commander of the belligerent warship has reason to suspect that the confidence of the commander of the convoy has been abused, he communicates his suspicions to him. In such a case it is for the commander of the convoy alone to investigate the matter. He must record the result of such investigation in a report, of which a copy is handed to the officer of the warship. If, in the opinion of the commander of the convoy, the facts shown in the report justify the capture of one or more vessels, the protection of the convoy must be withdrawn from such vessels.

CHAPTER VIII.

Resistance to Search.

63. Forcible resistance to the legitimate exercise of the right of stoppage, search, and capture, involves in all cases the condemnation of the vessel. The cargo is liable to the same treatment as the cargo of an enemy vessel. Goods belonging to the master or owner of the vessel are treated as enemy goods.

CHAPTER IX.

Compensation.

64. If the capture of a vessel or of goods is not upheld by the Prize Court, or if the prize is released without any judgment being given, the parties interested have the right to compensation, unless there were good reasons for capturing the vessel or goods.

Final Provisions.

65. The provisions of the present Declaration must be treated as a whole, and cannot be separated.

66. The Signatory Powers undertake to ensure the mutual observance of the rules contained in the present Declaration in any war in which all the belligerents are parties thereto. They will therefore issue the necessary instructions to their authorities and to their armed forces, and will take such measures as may be required in order to ensure that it will be applied by their courts, and more particularly by their Prize Courts.

67. The present Declaration shall be ratified as soon as possible.

The ratifications shall be deposited in London.

The first deposit of ratifications shall be recorded in a Protocol signed by the Representatives of the Powers taking part therein, and by His Britannic Majesty's Principal Secretary of State for Foreign Affairs.

The subsequent deposits of ratifications shall be made by means of a written notification addressed to the British Government, and accompanied by the instrument of ratification.

A duly certified copy of the Protocol relating to the first deposit of ratifications, and of the notifications mentioned in the preceding paragraph, as well as of the instruments of ratification which accompany them, shall be immediately sent by the British Government, through the diplomatic channel, to the Signatory Powers. The said Government shall, in the cases contemplated in the preceding paragraph, inform them at the same time of the date on which it received the notification.

68. The present Declaration shall take effect, in the case of the Powers which were parties to the first deposit of ratifications, sixty days after the date of the Protocol recording such deposit, and, in the case of the Powers which shall ratify subsequently, sixty days after the notification of their ratification shall have been received by the British Government.

69. In the event of one of the Signatory Powers wishing to denounce the present Declaration, such denunciation can only be made to take effect at the end of a period of twelve years, beginning sixty days after the first deposit of ratifications, and, after that time, at the end of successive periods of six years, of which the first will begin at the end of the period of twelve years.

Such denunciation must be notified in writing, at least one year in advance to the British Government, which shall inform all the other Powers.

It will only operate in respect of the denouncing Power.

70. The Powers represented at the London Naval Conference attach particular importance to the general recognition of the rules which they have adopted, and therefore express the hope that the Powers which were not represented there will accede to the present Declaration. They request the British Government to invite them to do so.

A Power which desires to accede shall notify its intention in writing to the British Government, and transmit simultaneously the act of accession, which will be deposited in the archives of the said Government.

The said Government shall forthwith transmit to all the other Powers a duly certified copy of the notification, together with the act of accession, and communicate the date on which such notification was received. The accession takes effect sixty days after such date.

In respect of all matters concerning this Declaration, acceding Powers shall be on the same footing as the Signatory Powers.

71. The present Declaration, which bears the date of the 26th February, 1909, may be signed in London up till the 30th June, 1909, by the Plenipotentiaries of the Powers represented at the Naval Conference.

GPSR Compliance

The European Union's (EU) General Product Safety Regulation (GPSR) is a set of rules that requires consumer products to be safe and our obligations to ensure this.

If you have any concerns about our products, you can contact us on ProductSafety@springernature.com

In case Publisher is established outside the EU, the EU authorized representative is:

Springer Nature Customer Service Center GmbH
Europaplatz 3
69115 Heidelberg, Germany

Batch number: 10830935

Printed by Printforce, the Netherlands